KICK-ASS

D1427198

MARK MILLAR
WRITER AND CO-CREATOR

JOHN ROMITA JR.
PENCILLER AND CO-CREATOR

TOM PALMER
INKS

DEAN WHITE
COLOURS

CHRIS ELIOPOULOS
LETTERS

JOHN BARBER
ORIGINAL SERIES EDITOR

TITAN BOOKS

FOR ICON

MICHAEL HORWITZ
ASSISTANT EDITOR

JEFF YOUNGQUIST
SENIOR EDITOR, SPECIAL PROJECTS

ANTHONY DIAL & IRENE LEE
PRODUCTION

DAVID GABRIEL
SENIOR VICE PRESIDENT OF SALES

DAVID BOGART
SVP OF BUSINESS AFFAIRS & TALENT MANAGEMENT

JOE QUESADA
EDITOR IN CHIEF

DAN BUCKLEY
PUBLISHER

ALAN FINE
EXECUTIVE PRODUCER

KICK-ASS
ISBN: 9780857681027

Published by Titan Books
A division of Titan Publishing Group Ltd.
144 Southwark Street
London
SE1 0UP

Kick-Ass comic strip © 2010 Mark Millar and John S. Romita.

A CIP catalogue record for this title is available from the British Library.

This edition: September 2010
10 9 8 7 6 5 4 3 2
First published in the UK March 2010. Revised and expanded September 2010.

Printed in Spain.

What did you think of this book? We love to hear from our readers. Please email us at: readerfeedback@titanemail.com, or write to us at the above address.

To receive advance information, news, competitions, and exclusive offers online, please sign up for the Titan newsletter on our website: **www.titanbooks.com**

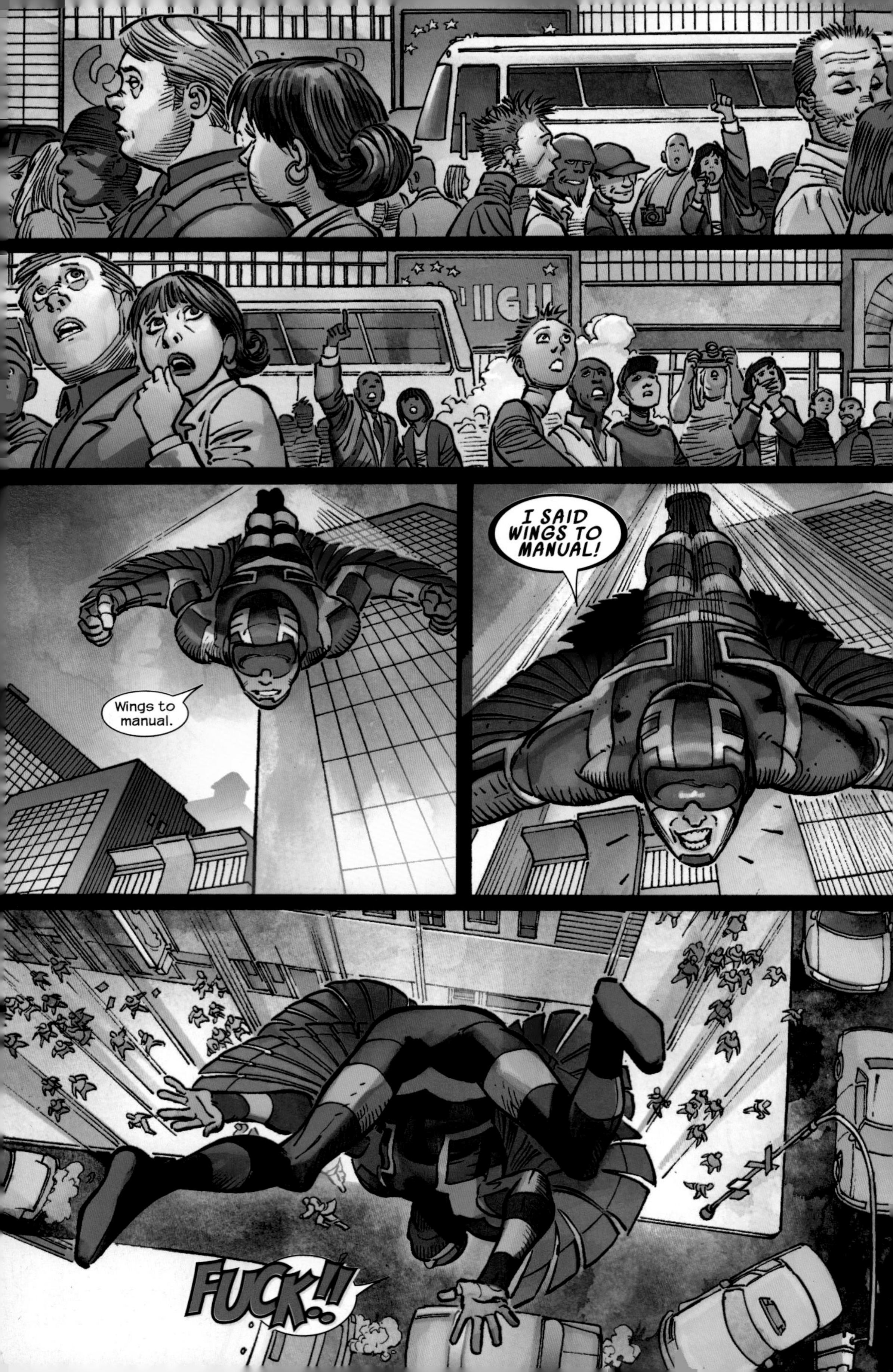
Wings to manual.
I SAID WINGS TO MANUAL!
FUCK!!

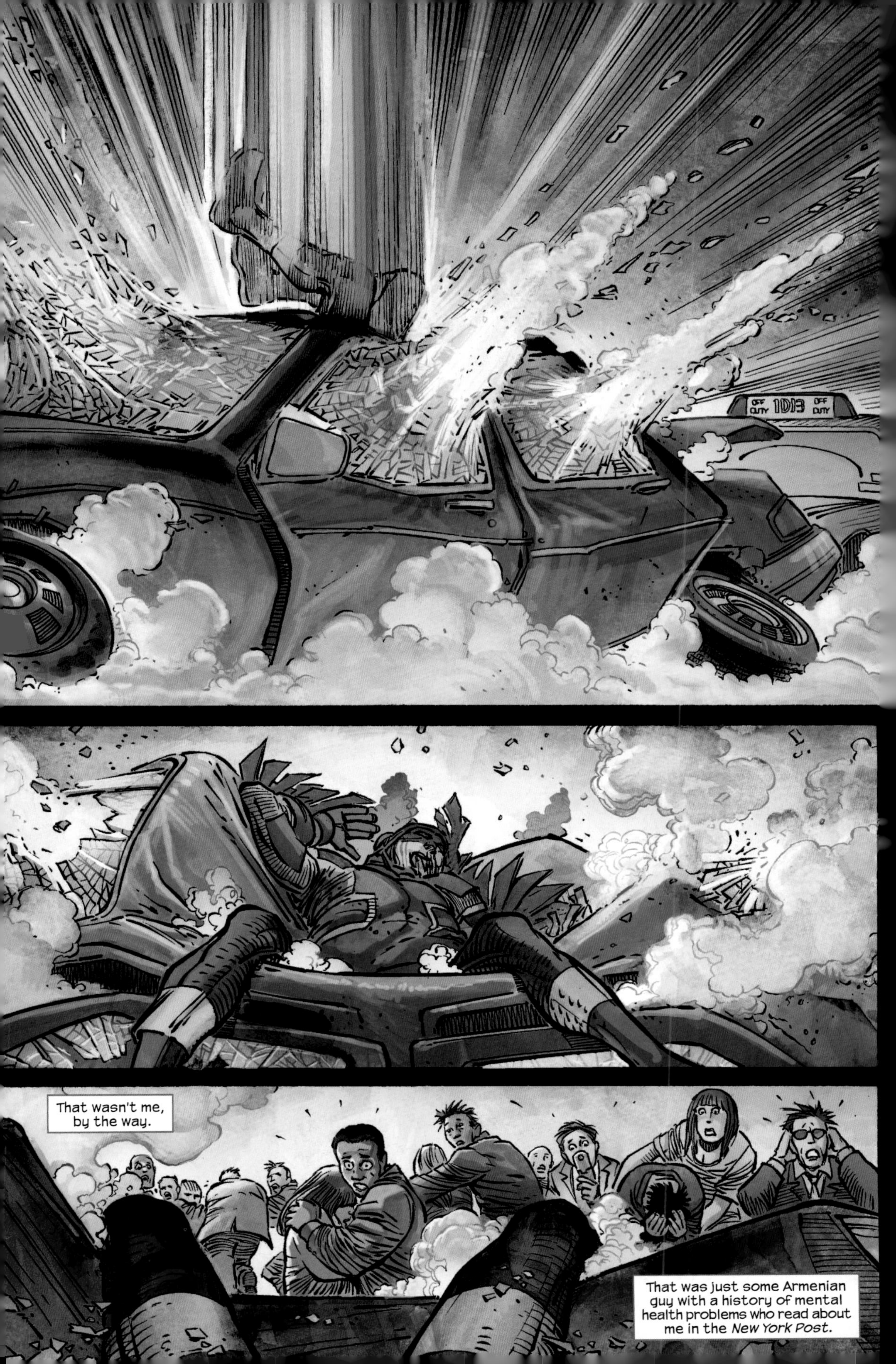
OFF DUTY 1D13 OFF DUTY
That wasn't me, by the way.
That was just some Armenian guy with a history of mental health problems who read about me in the *New York Post*.

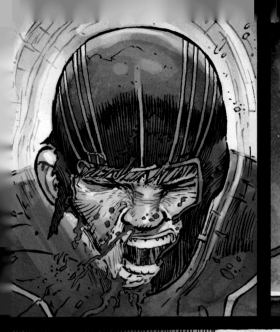

I'm the guy with the electrodes attached to his testicles.

Obviously, this isn't what I had in mind when I first pulled on the mask. I thought it would be more leaping over rooftops and pithy put-downs to purse snatchers.

But this is the reality of the situation. This is what happens when you mess with bad people.

YOU COST US MONEY, YOU LITTLE FUCK!

But perhaps I'm getting ahead of myself. Perhaps it's wise to just start at the beginning...

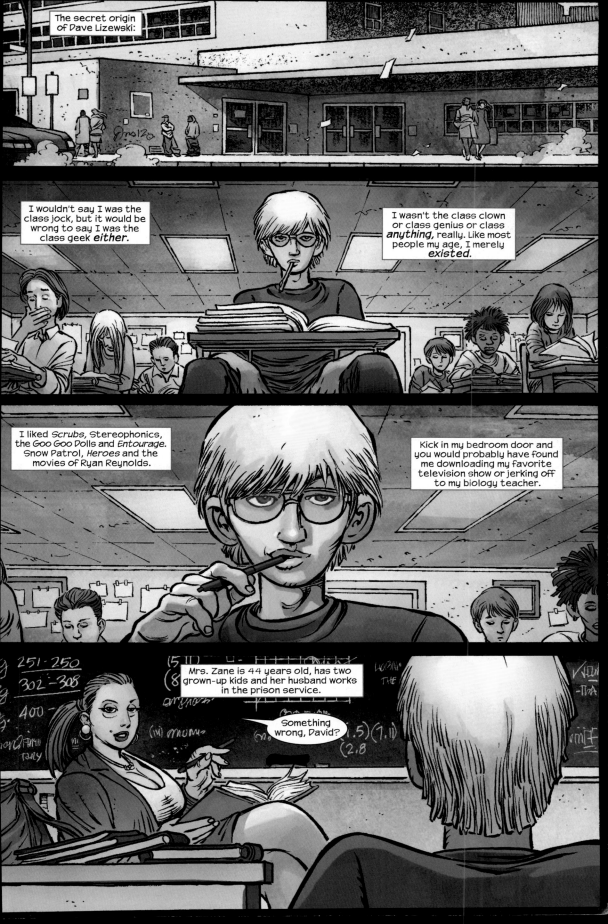

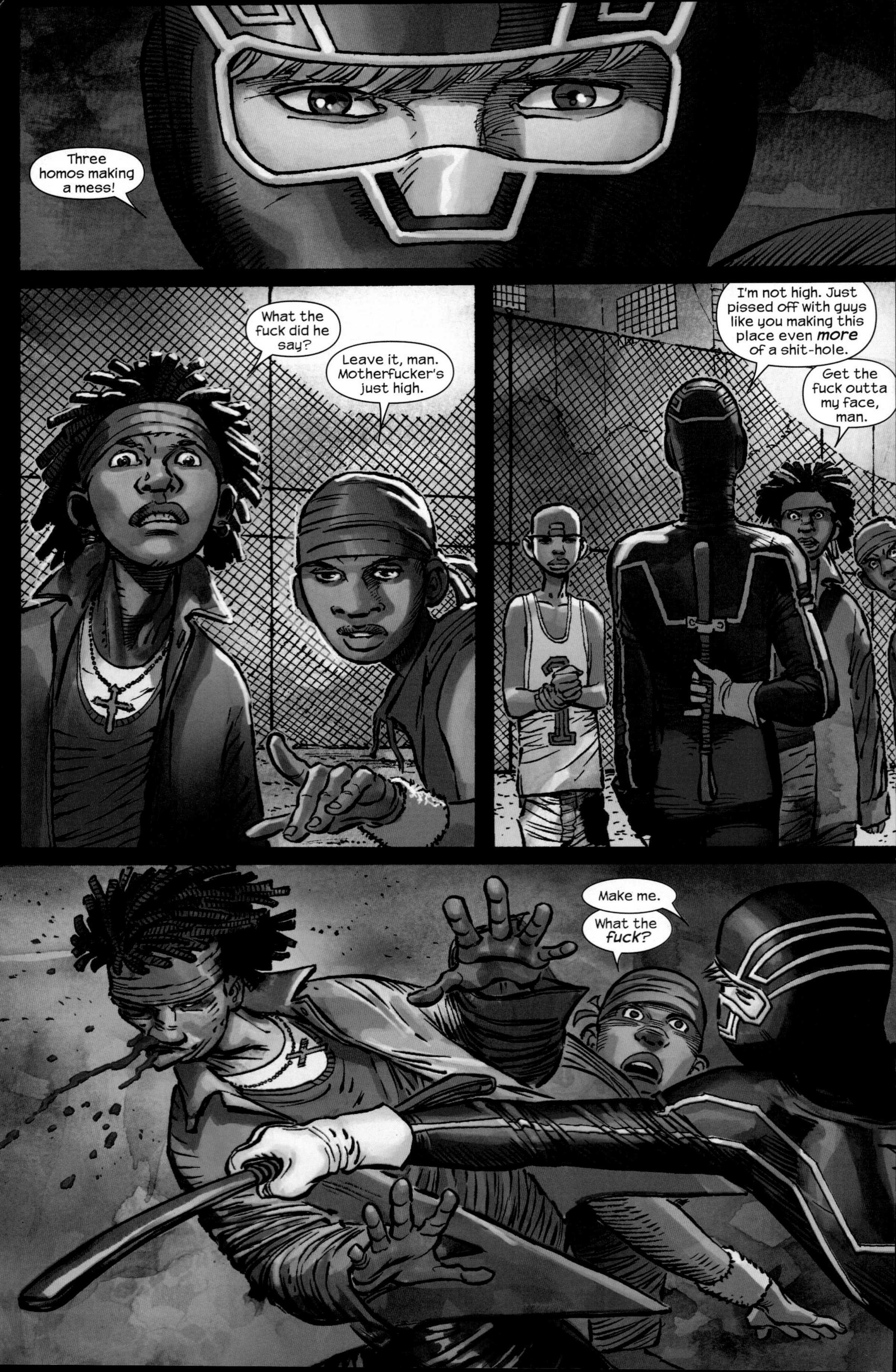

Three homos making a mess!
What the fuck did he say?
Leave it, man. Motherfucker's just high.
I'm not high. Just pissed off with guys like you making this place even *more* of a shit-hole.
Get the fuck outta my face, man.
Make me.
What the *fuck*?

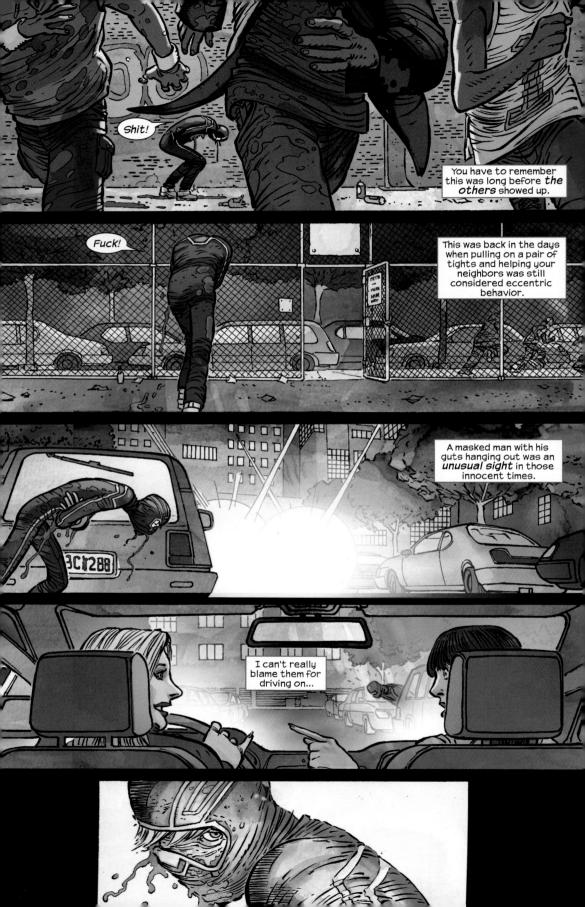

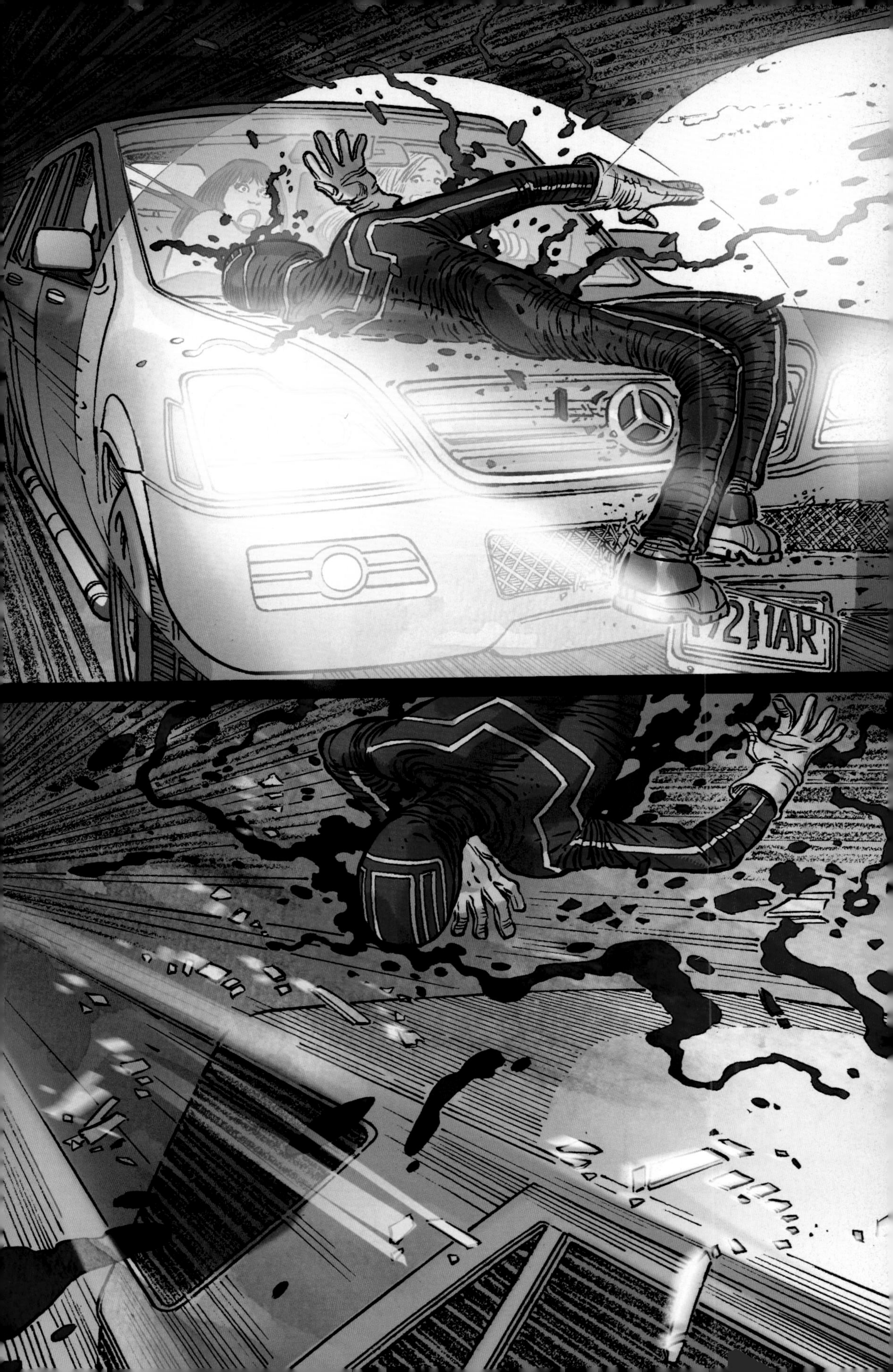

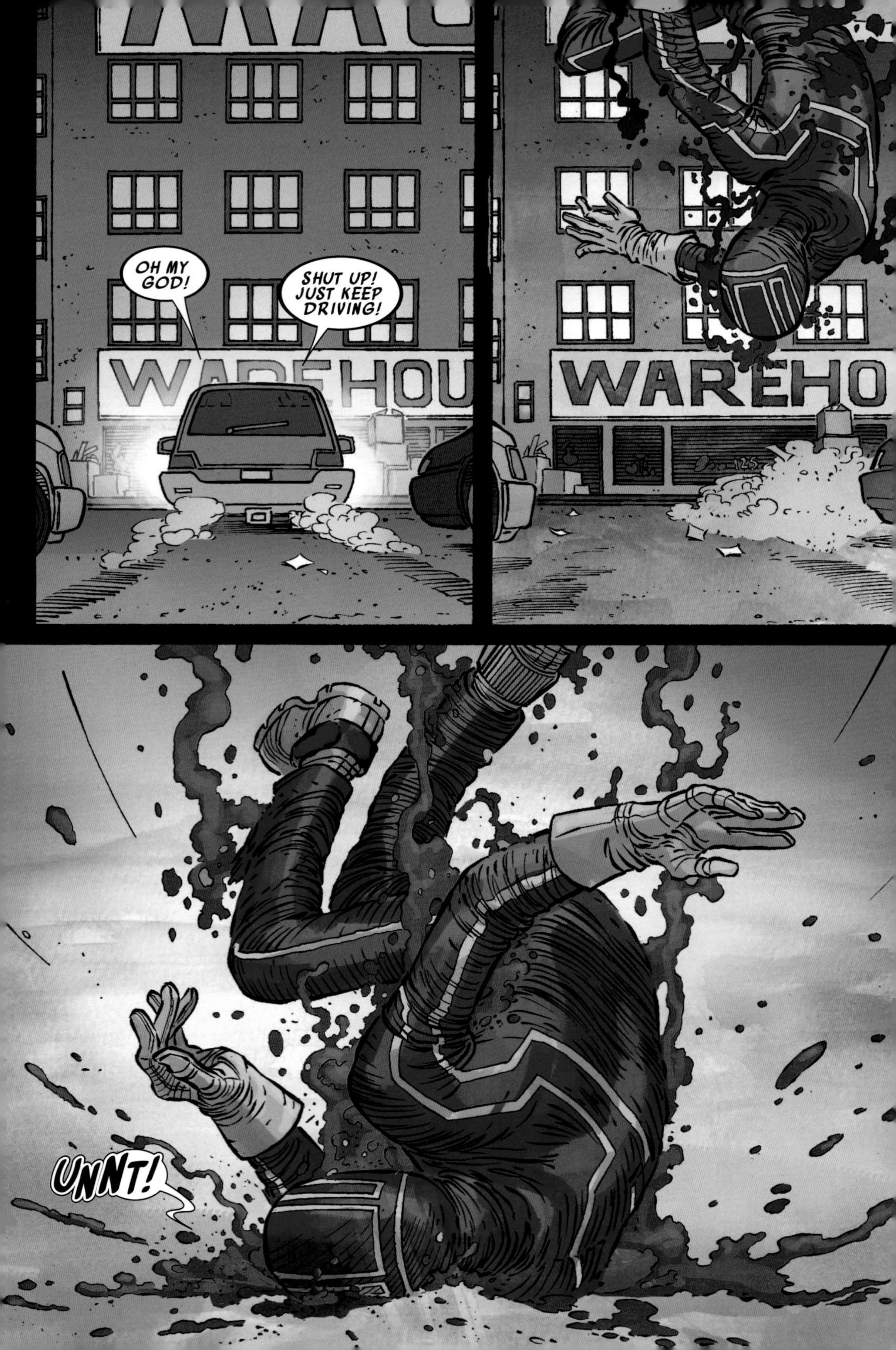
OH MY GOD!
SHUT UP! JUST KEEP DRIVING!
WAREHOU
WAREHO
UNNT!

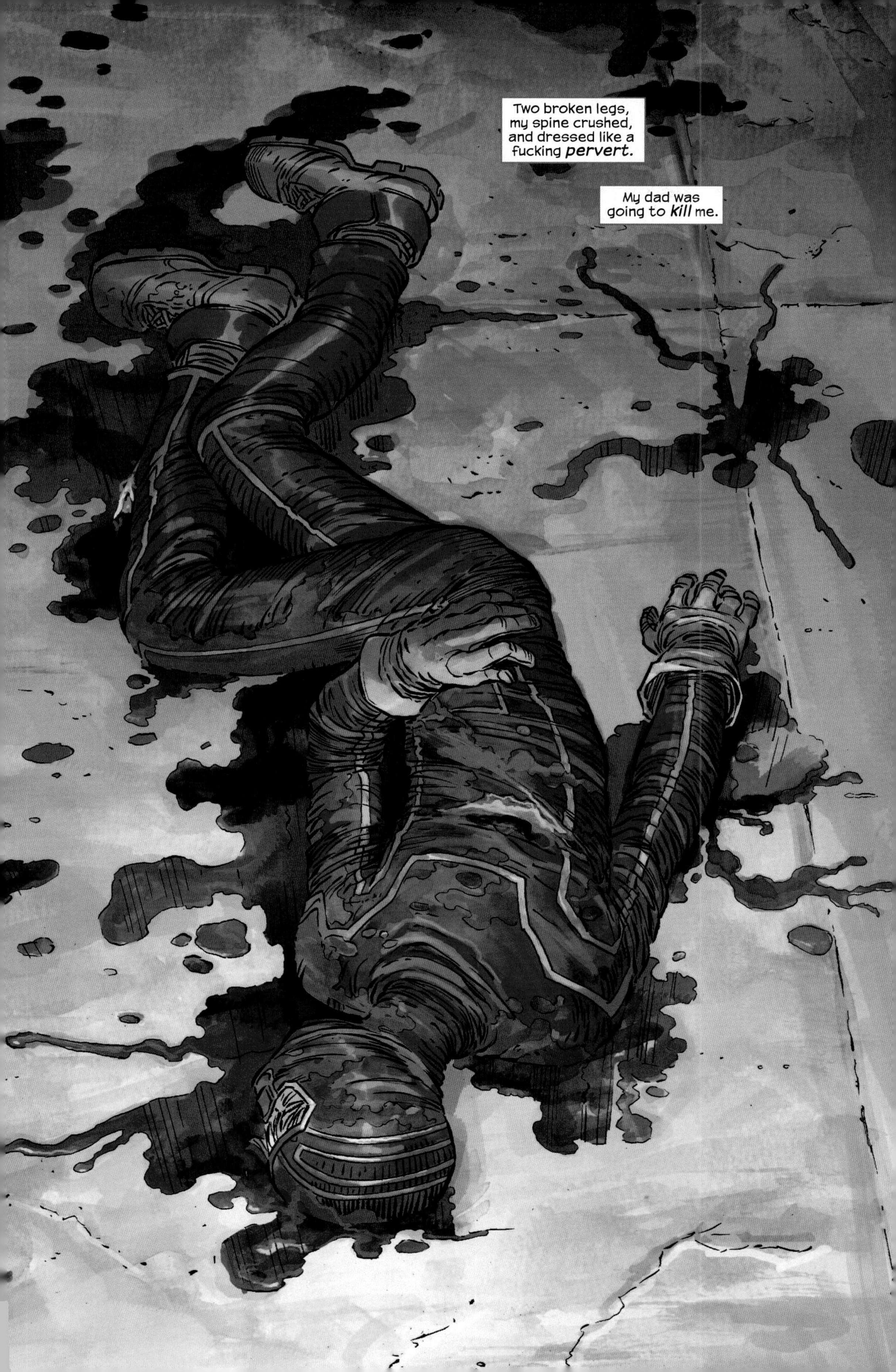
Two broken legs, my spine crushed, and dressed like a fucking *pervert.*
My dad was going to *kill* me.

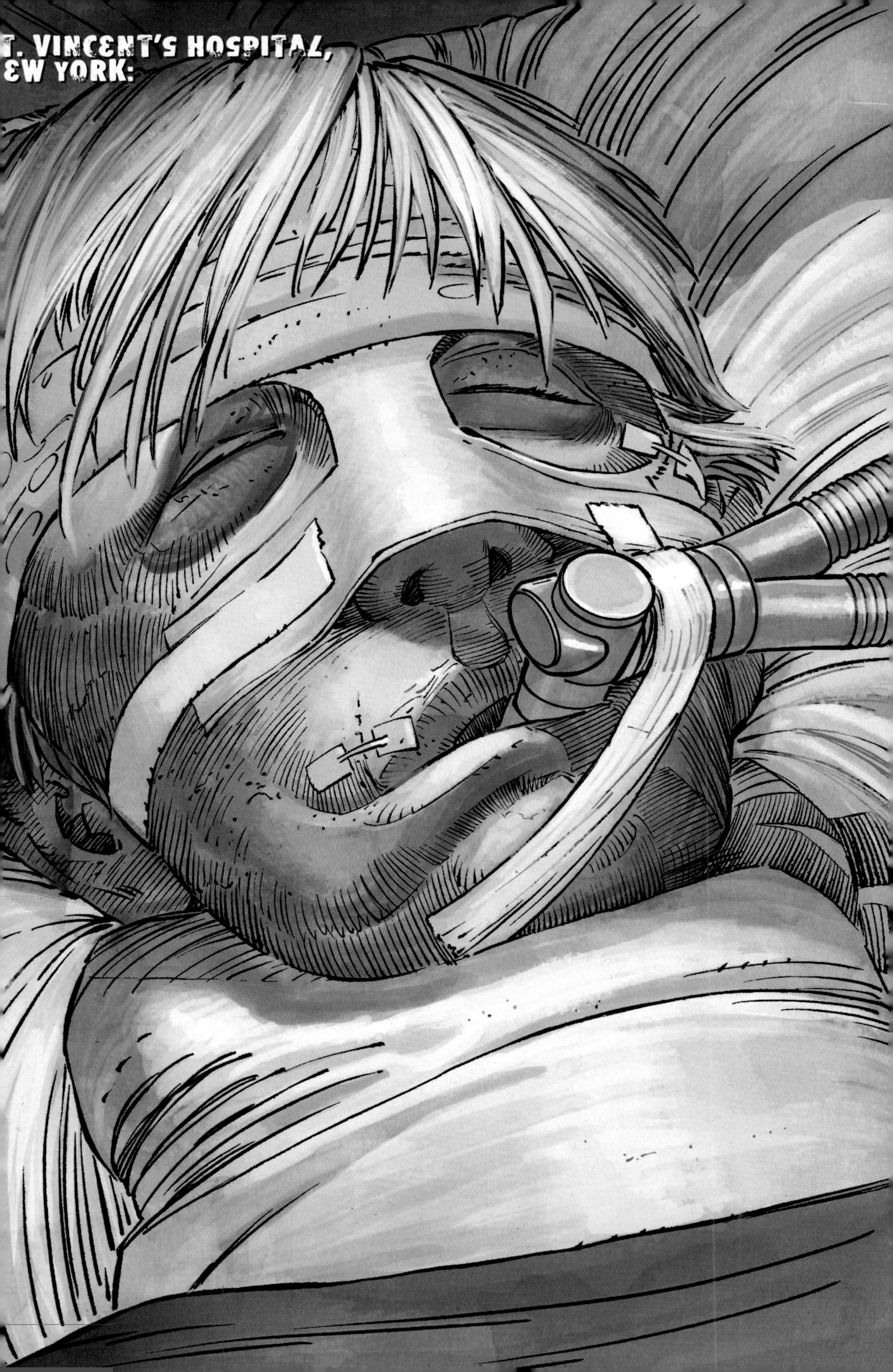
T. VINCENT'S HOSPITAL,
EW YORK:

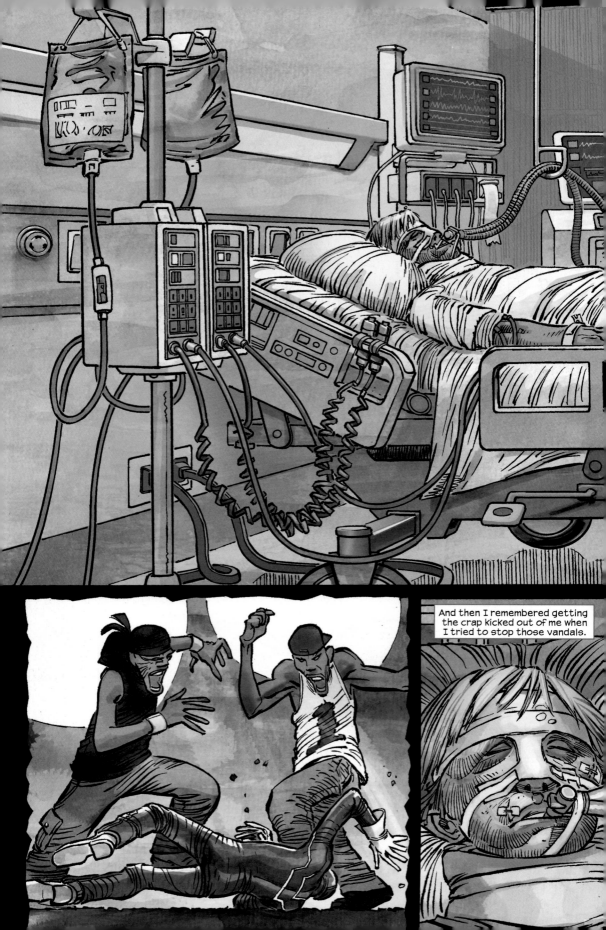

And then I remembered getting the crap kicked out of me when I tried to stop those vandals.

Two months later, I was allowed to go back to school again. Just a couple of days at first, but before long I was back full-time and hanging with my homies.

Yeah, I'm still in a lot of pain, but a wise man counts his blessings. I take fourteen different pills a day, but-- fuck--I wasn't letting those muggers put me in the ground.

Fuckin' A, John McClane. You are *awesome*.

That superhero shit just made me *angry* now...

...stupid, adolescent crap that had snatched six months of my stupid fucking life.

One night I got so angry I had a bonfire in the garden, burning all my old comic books with my idiotic plans and secret costume designs.

Fuck these guys! *Fuck* these comics! *Fuck* these stupid characters...

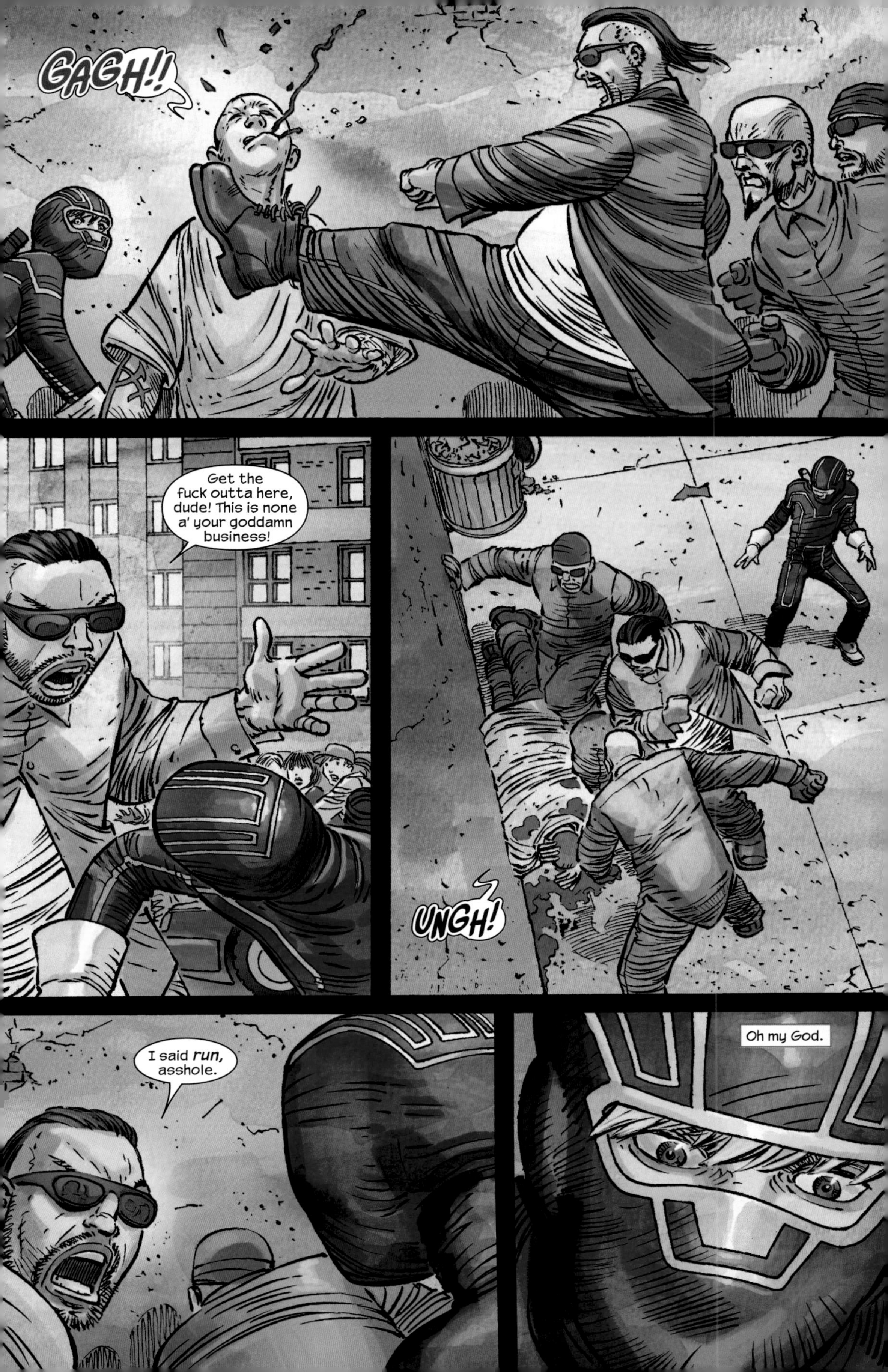
GAGH!!
Get the fuck outta here, dude! This is none a' your goddamn business!
UNGH!
I said *run*, asshole.
Oh my God.

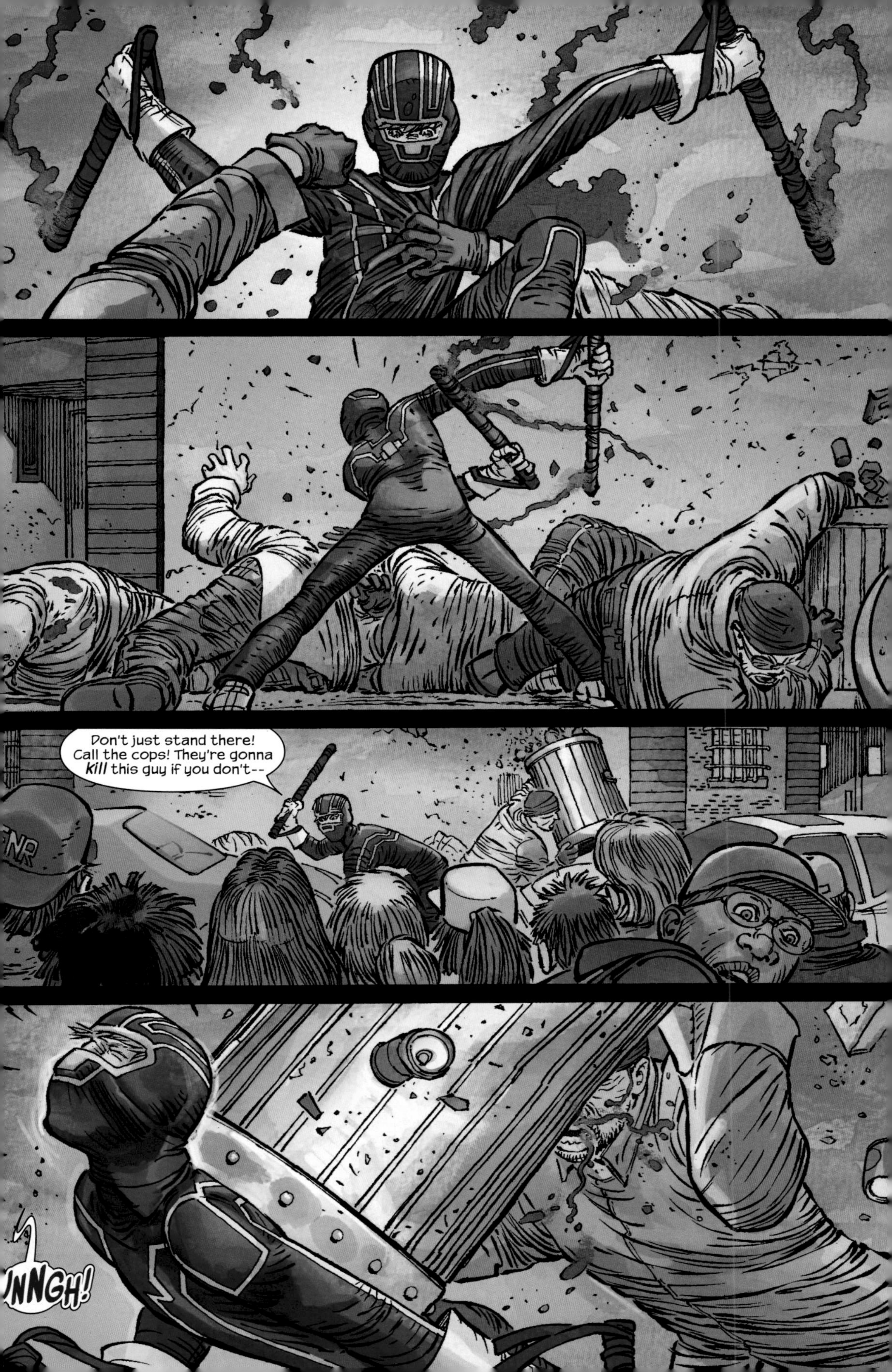

Don't just stand there! Call the cops! They're gonna *kill* this guy if you don't--
NNGH!

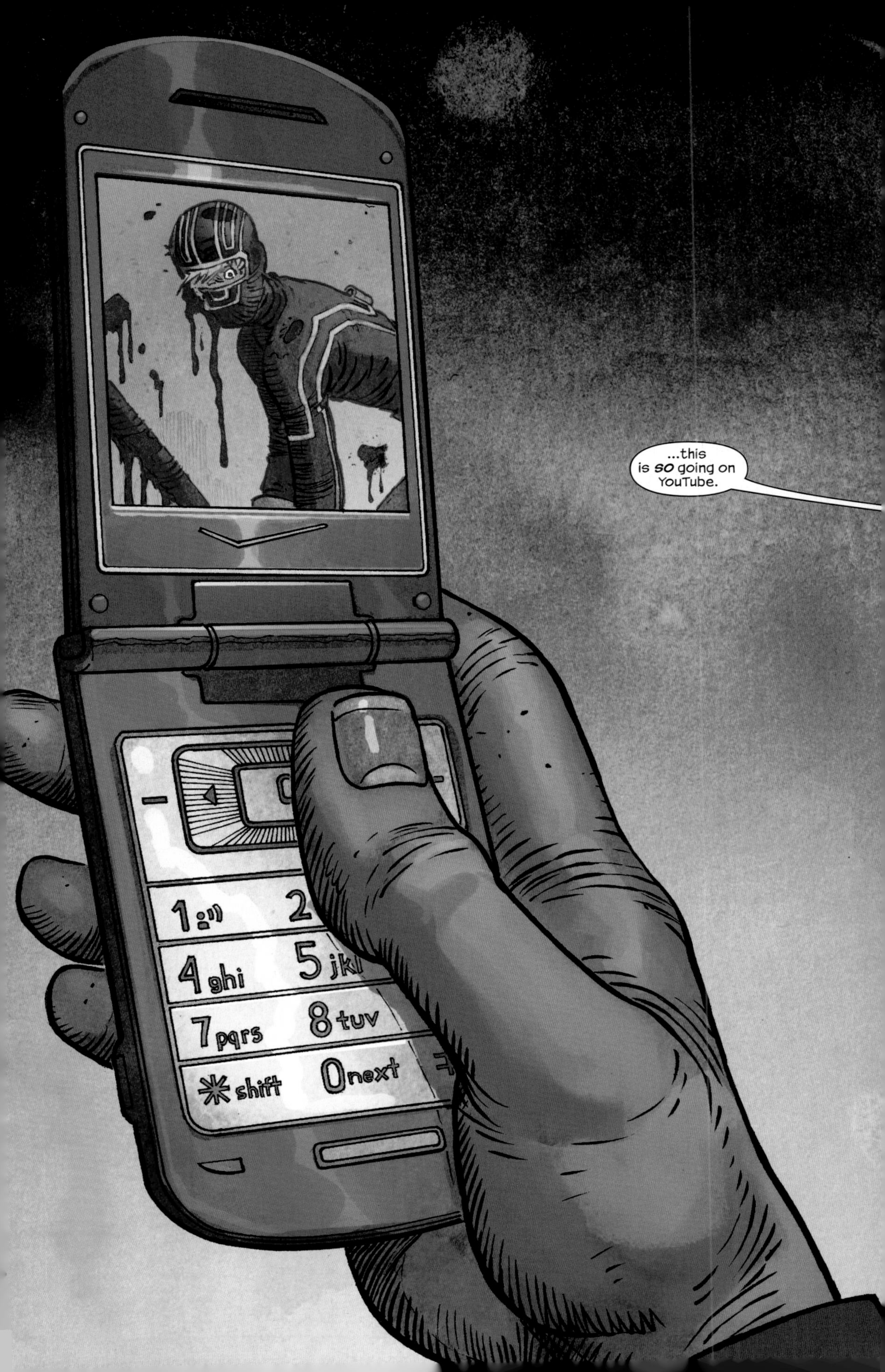
...this is *SO* going on YouTube.

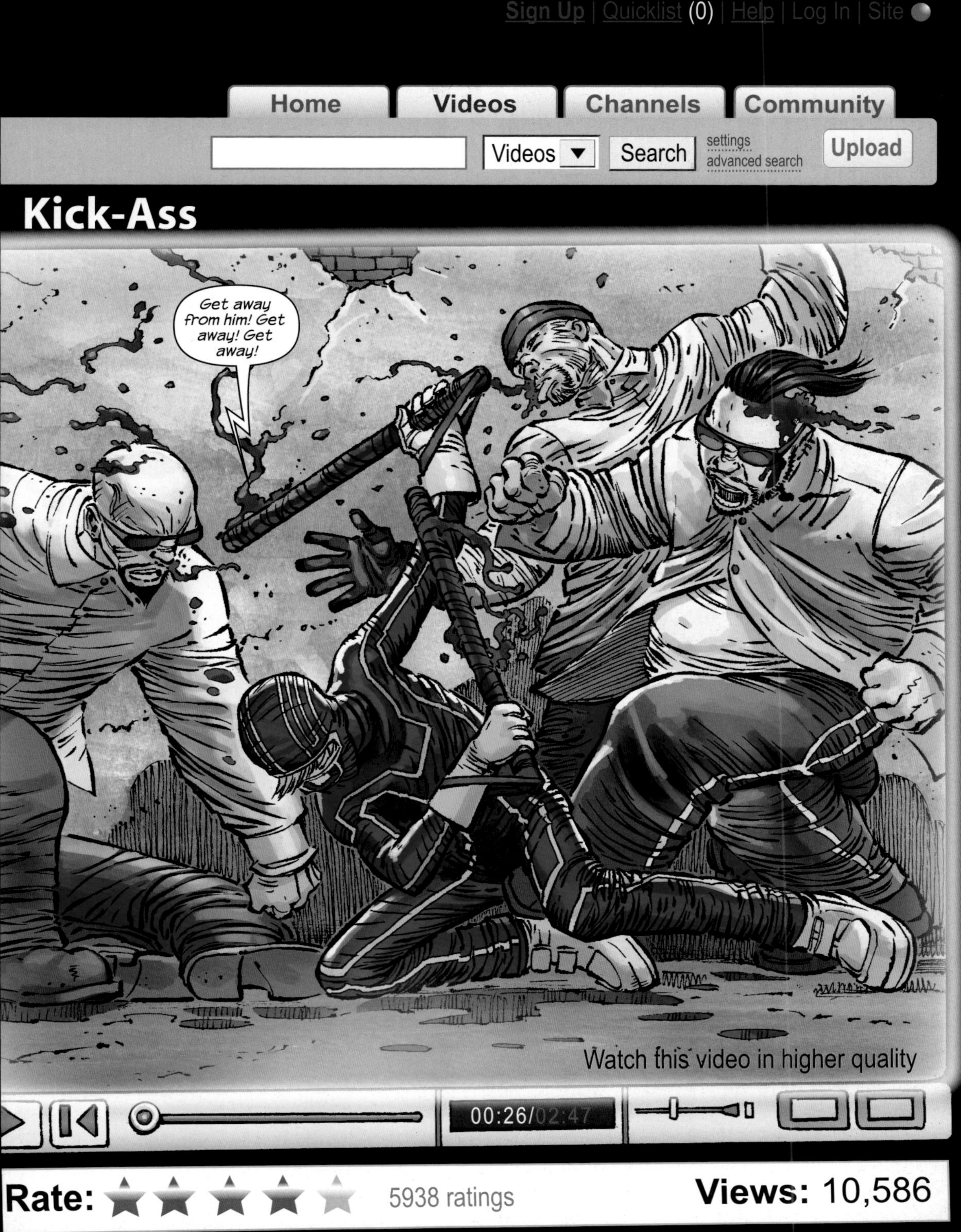
Sign Up | Quicklist (0) | Help | Log In | Site
Home
Videos
Channels
Community
Videos
Search
settings
advanced search
Upload
Kick-Ass
Get away from him! Get away! Get away!
Watch this video in higher quality
00:26/02:47
Rate:
5938 ratings
Views: 10,586

Oh, man. This is that video on the news last night. The guy who saved that kid from those *muggers*?

I'm not leaving him! You hear me?

I'm not leaving him...

This is fucking great. Is he really wearing a superhero costume?

You wouldn't believe how fast the celebrity thing happened.

up. The world's first real-life superhero.

Jay Leno said I was an *inspiration*. David Letterman gave me a *salute* at the end of his show.

I was a global sensation inside twenty-four hours. A bad-ass version of the Star Wars Kid. It was the greatest moment of my entire life...

KICK-ASS!

...and I finally had a name.

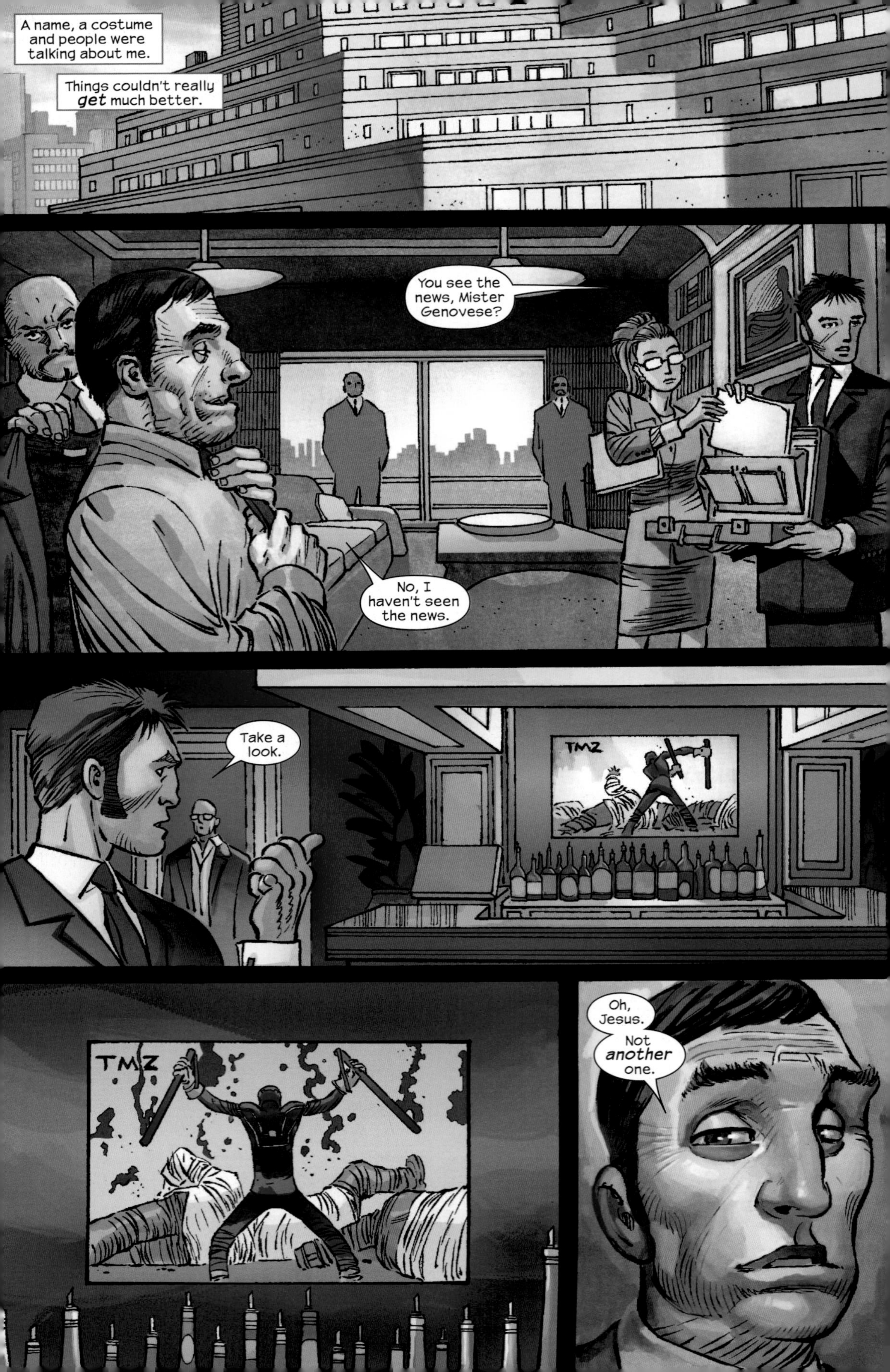
A name, a costume and people were talking about me.
Things couldn't really *get* much better.
You see the news, Mister Genovese?
No, I haven't seen the news.
Take a look.
TMZ
TMZ
Oh, Jesus.
Not *another* one.

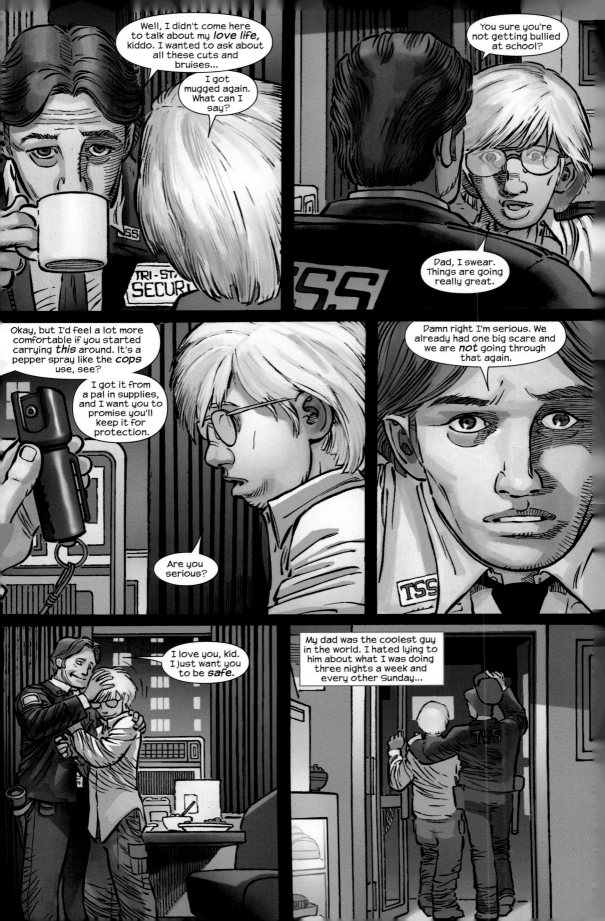

...but I'd have *opened a vein* if I didn't have that costume to hide inside.

Dave Lizewski had *eight* friends on MySpace and Kick-Ass had *thousands*.

I think that tells you everything you need to know.

These things are really far apart.

I figured that was the difference between comic books and real life. Real superheroes were down where the *action* was...

Kick-Ass!

Hey, dude!

WE LOVE YOU, YOU CRAZY MOTHER-FUCKER!

Cool!

I'd started a MySpace page so people with problems could get in touch and I could maybe help them out a little.

It seemed a more effective way of doing the job than just wandering around on patrol every night.

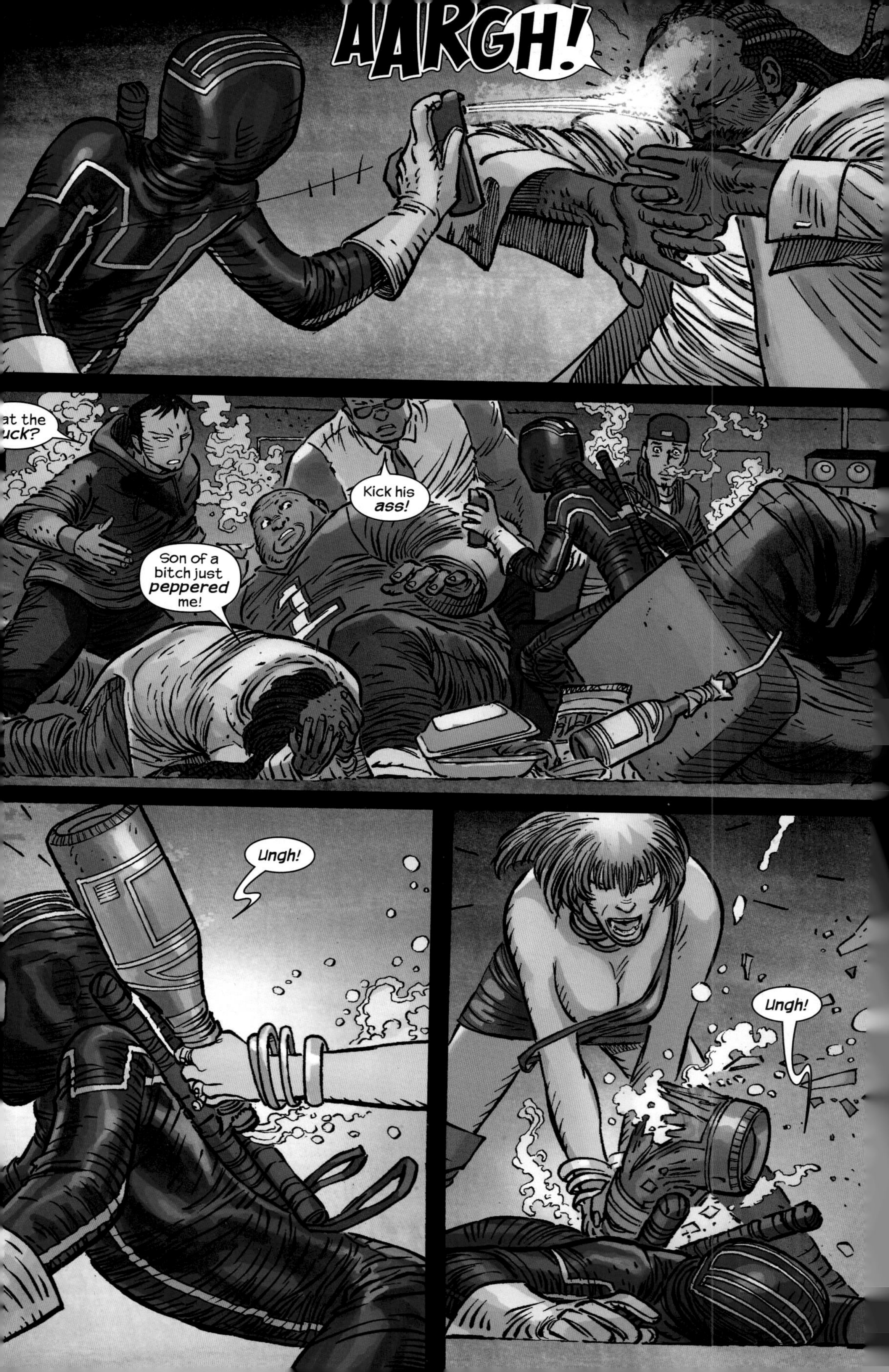
AARGH!
at the
uck?
Kick his ass!
Son of a bitch just peppered me!
Ungh!
Ungh!

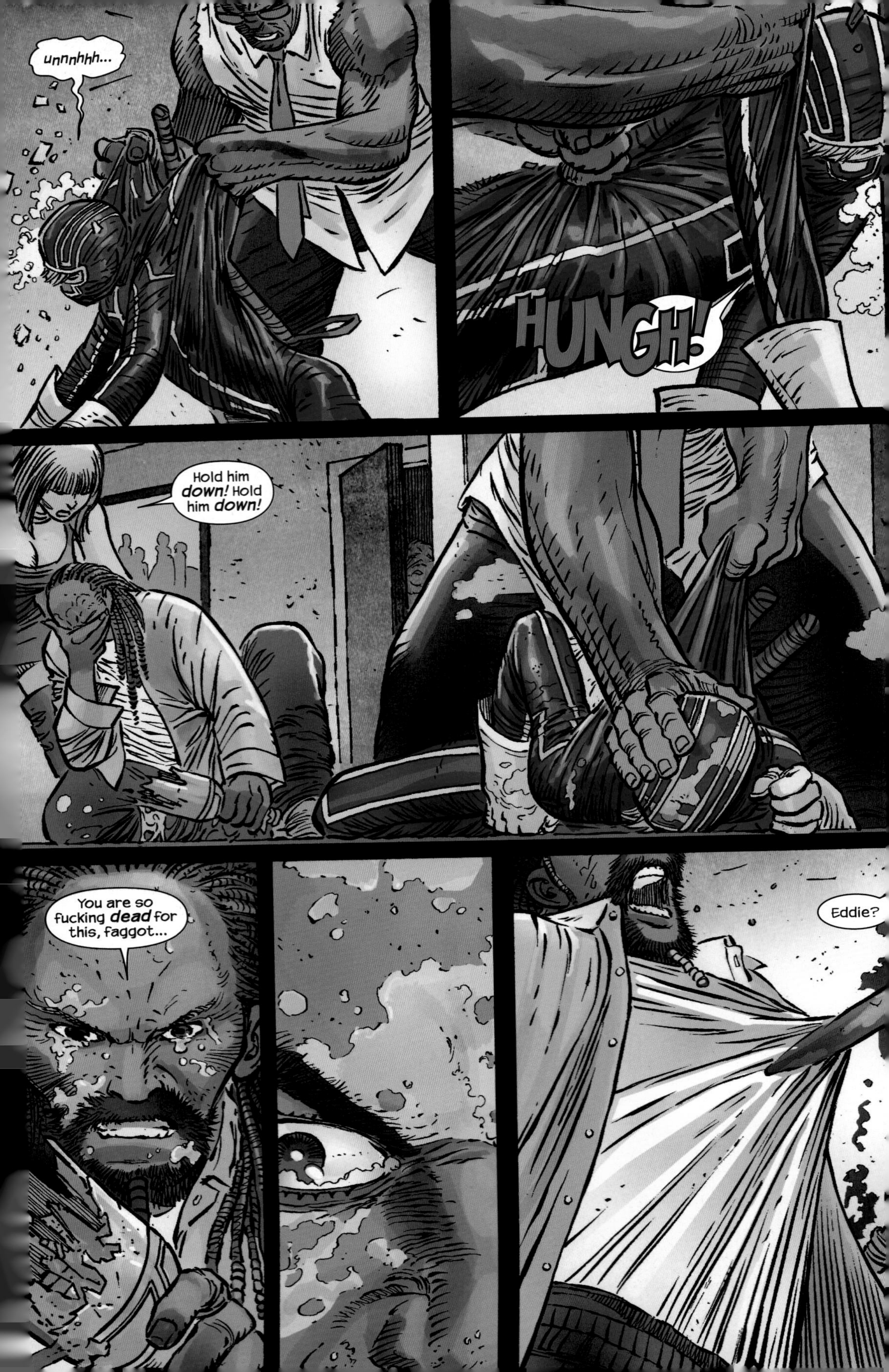
unnnhhh...
HUNGH!
Hold him *down!* Hold him *down!*
You are so fucking *dead* for this, faggot...
Eddie?

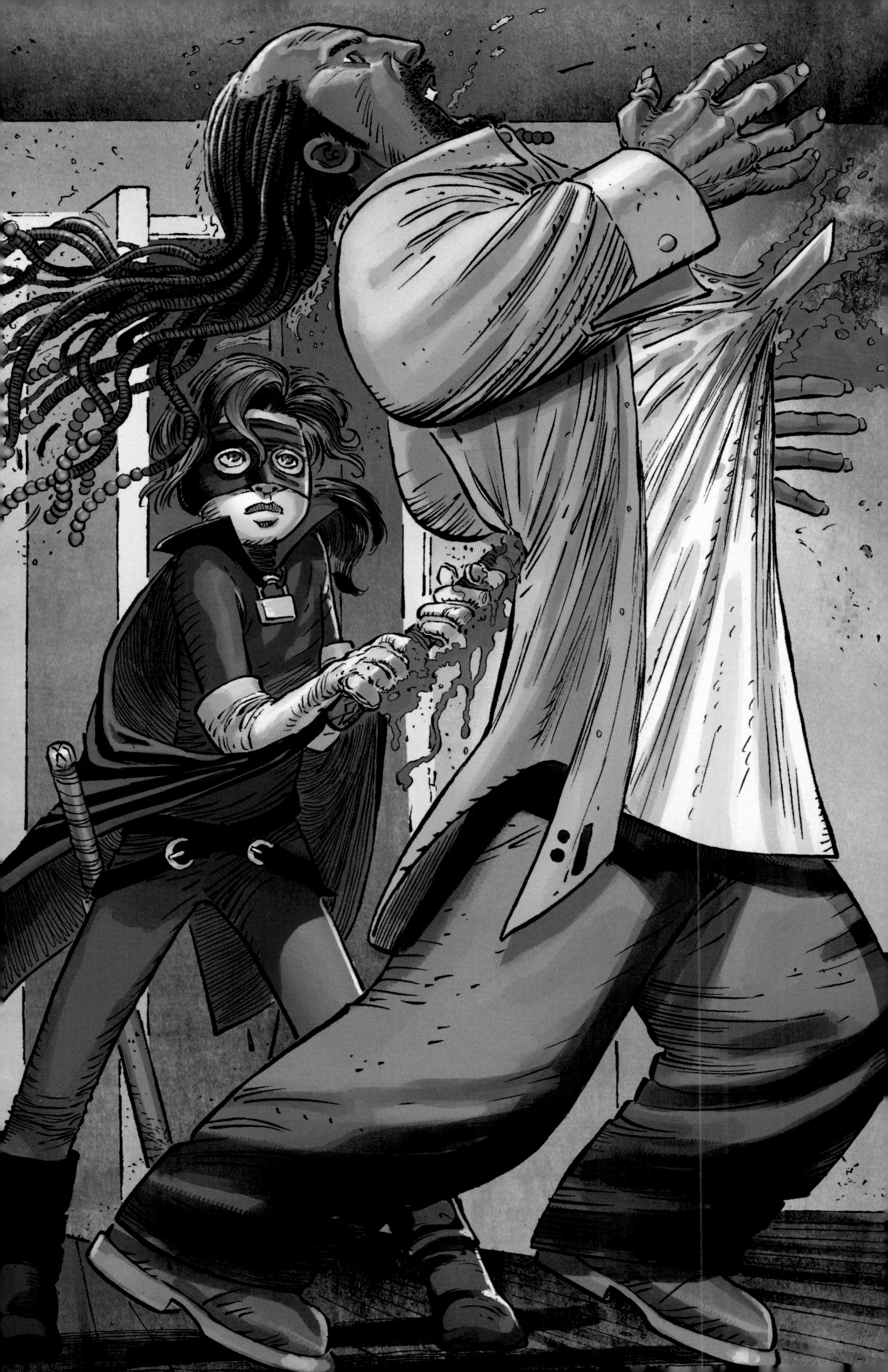

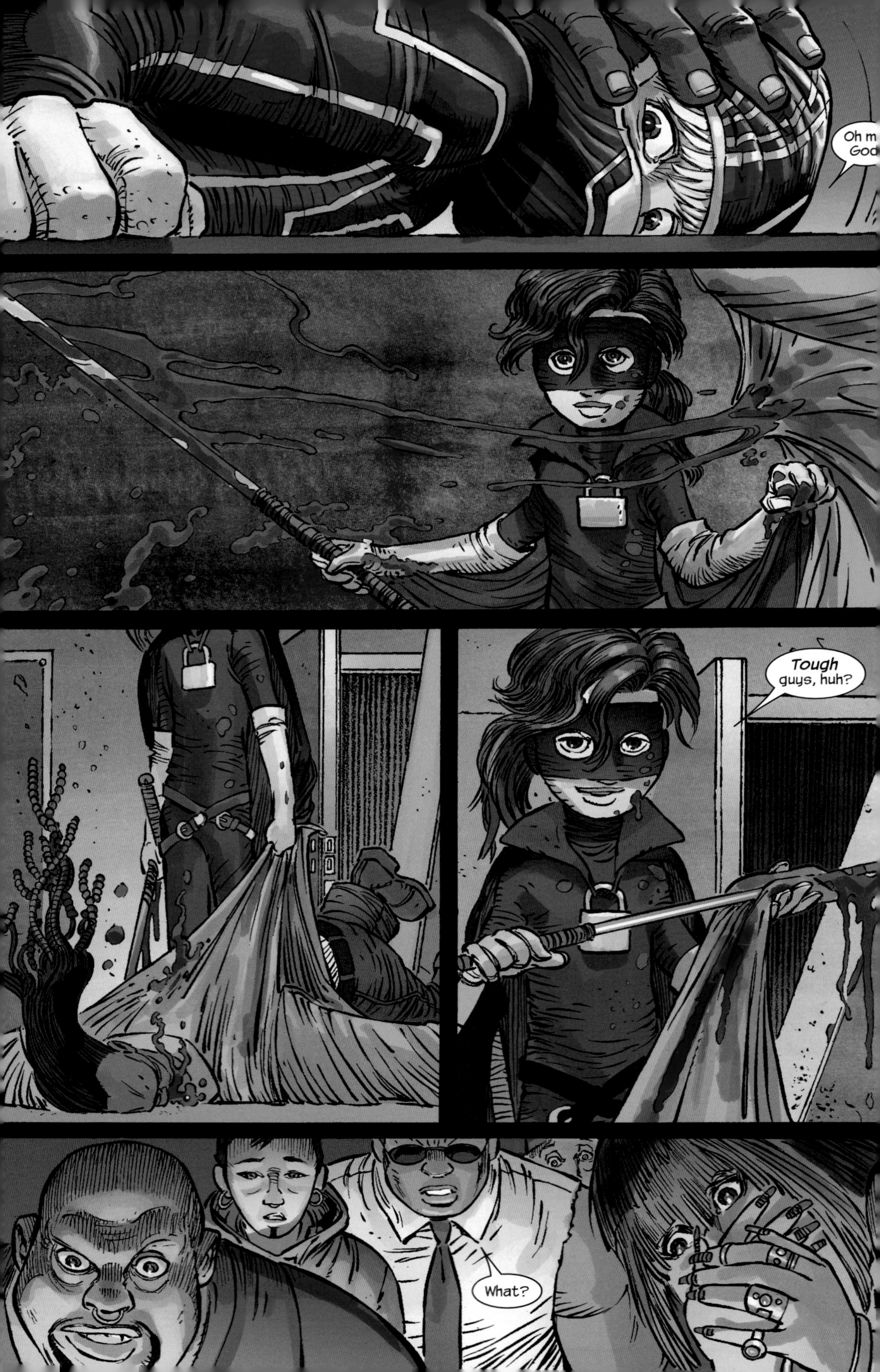
Oh m God
Tough guys, huh?
What?

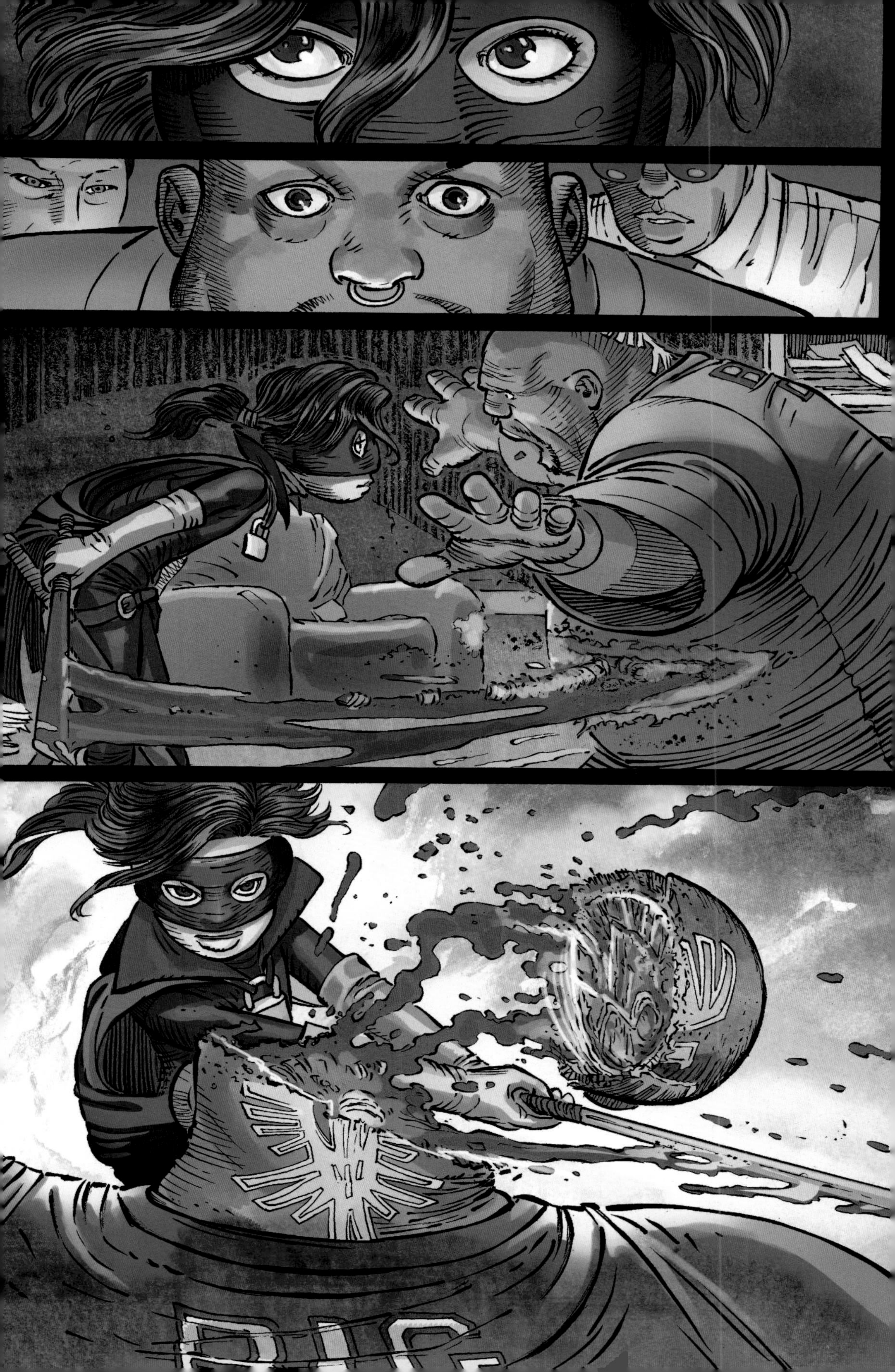

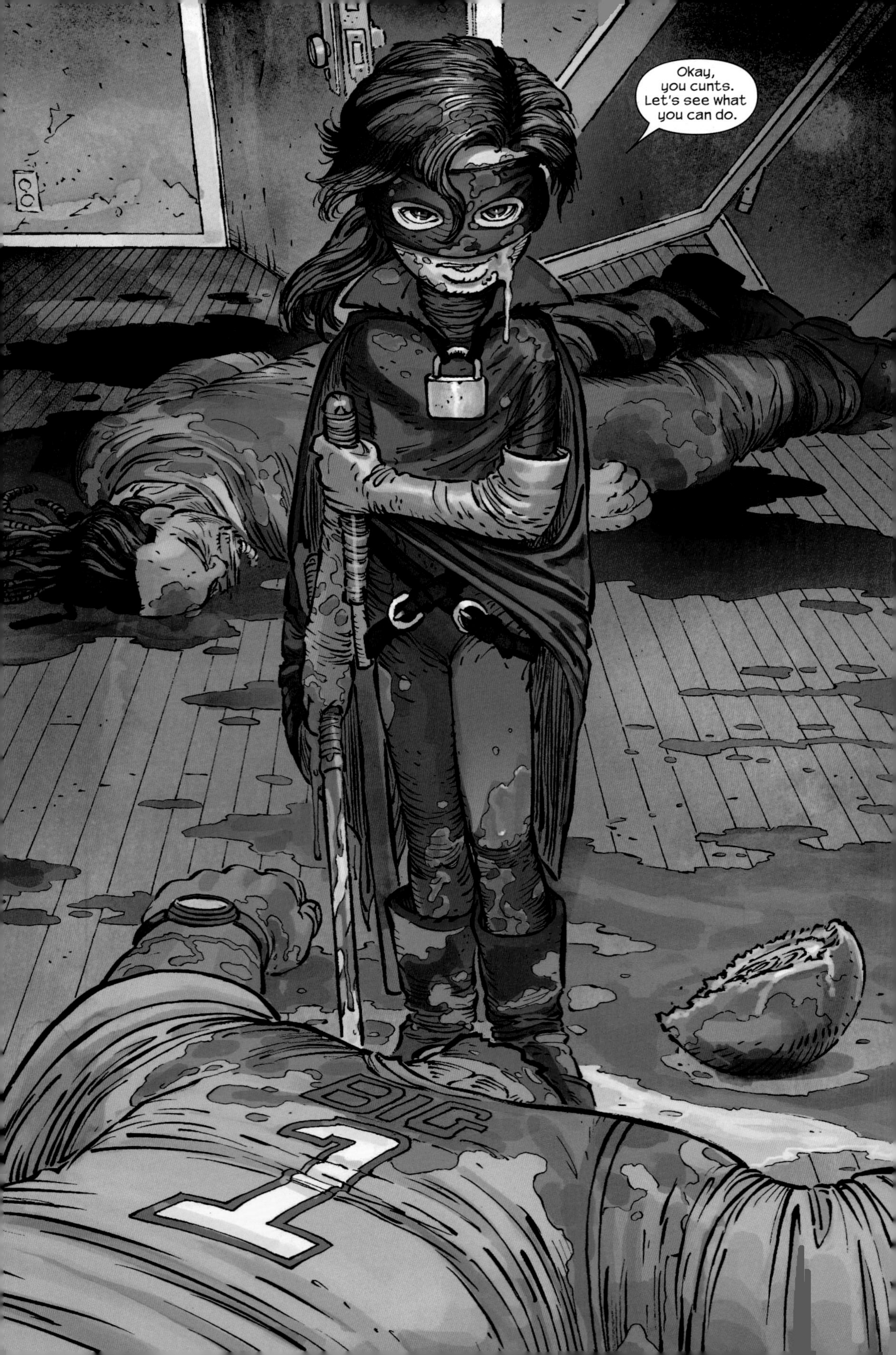
Okay, you cunts. Let's see what you can do.
BIG 1

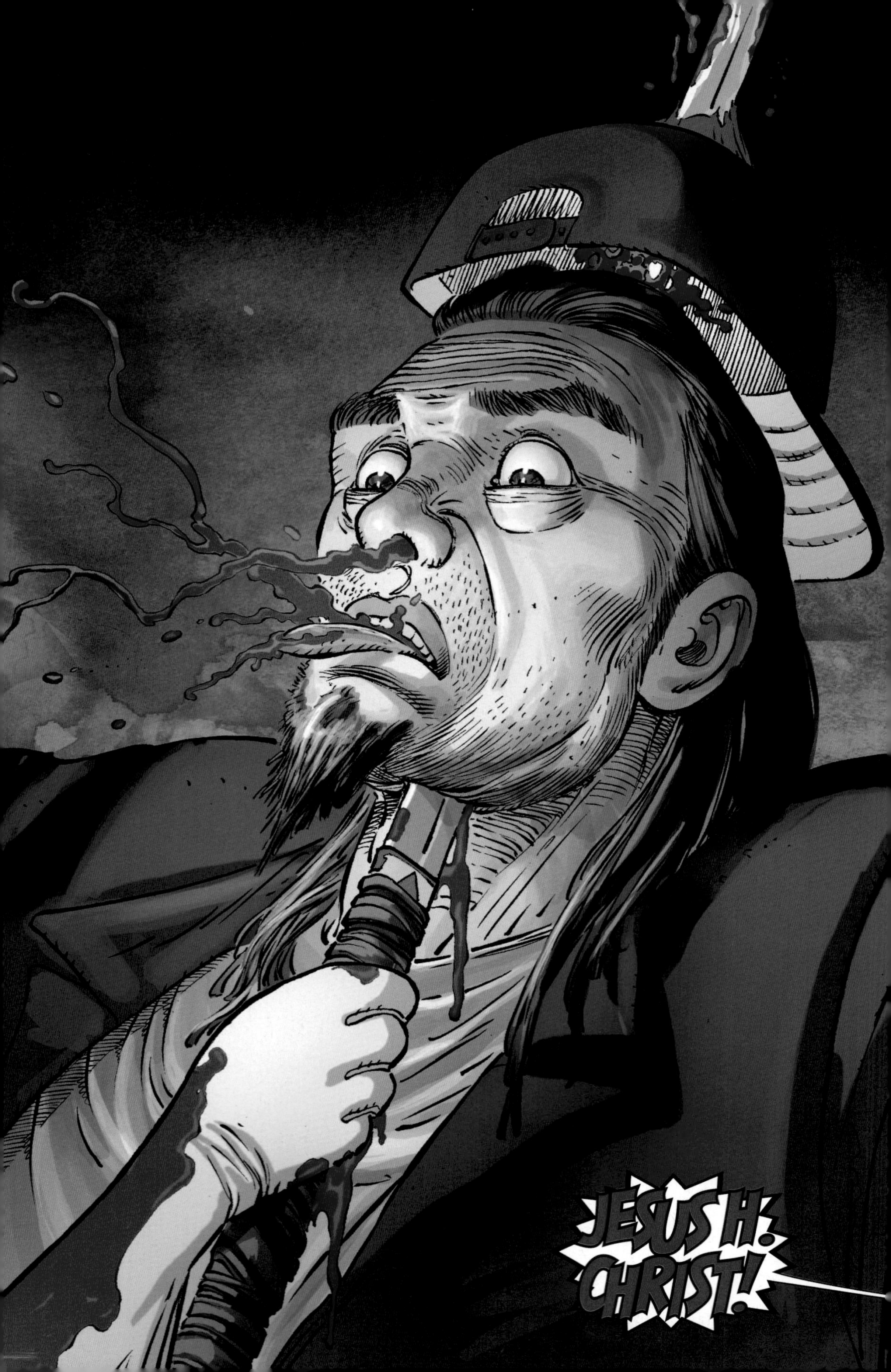
JESUS H. CHRIST!

She was like
John Rambo meets
Polly Pocket.

Dakota Fanning
crossed with
Death Wish 4.

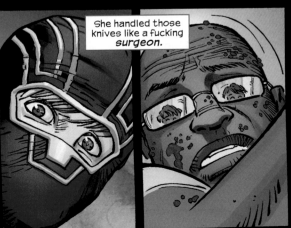

She handled those
knives like a fucking
surgeon.

I still can't
believe she was
only *ten...*

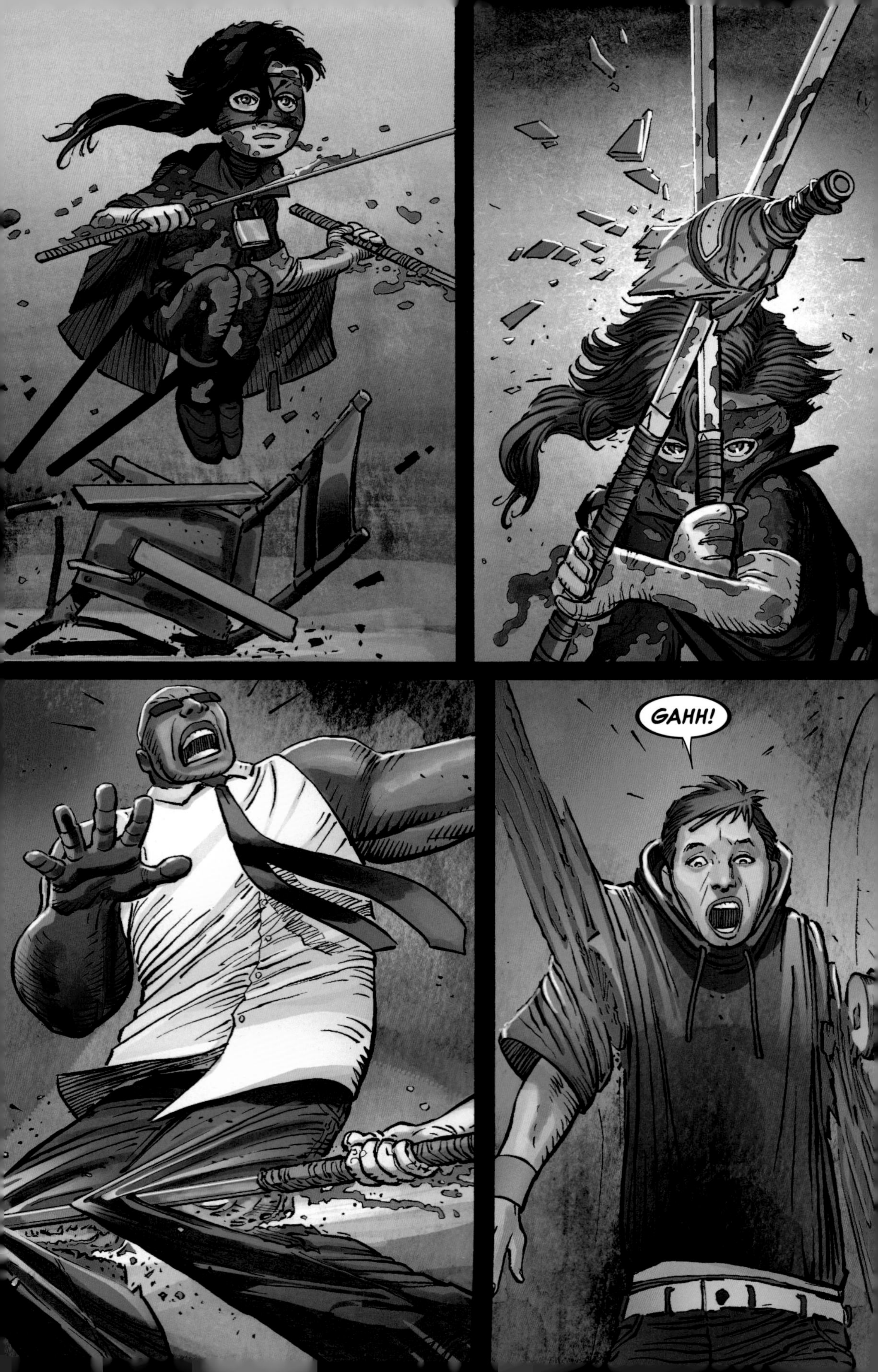
GAHH!

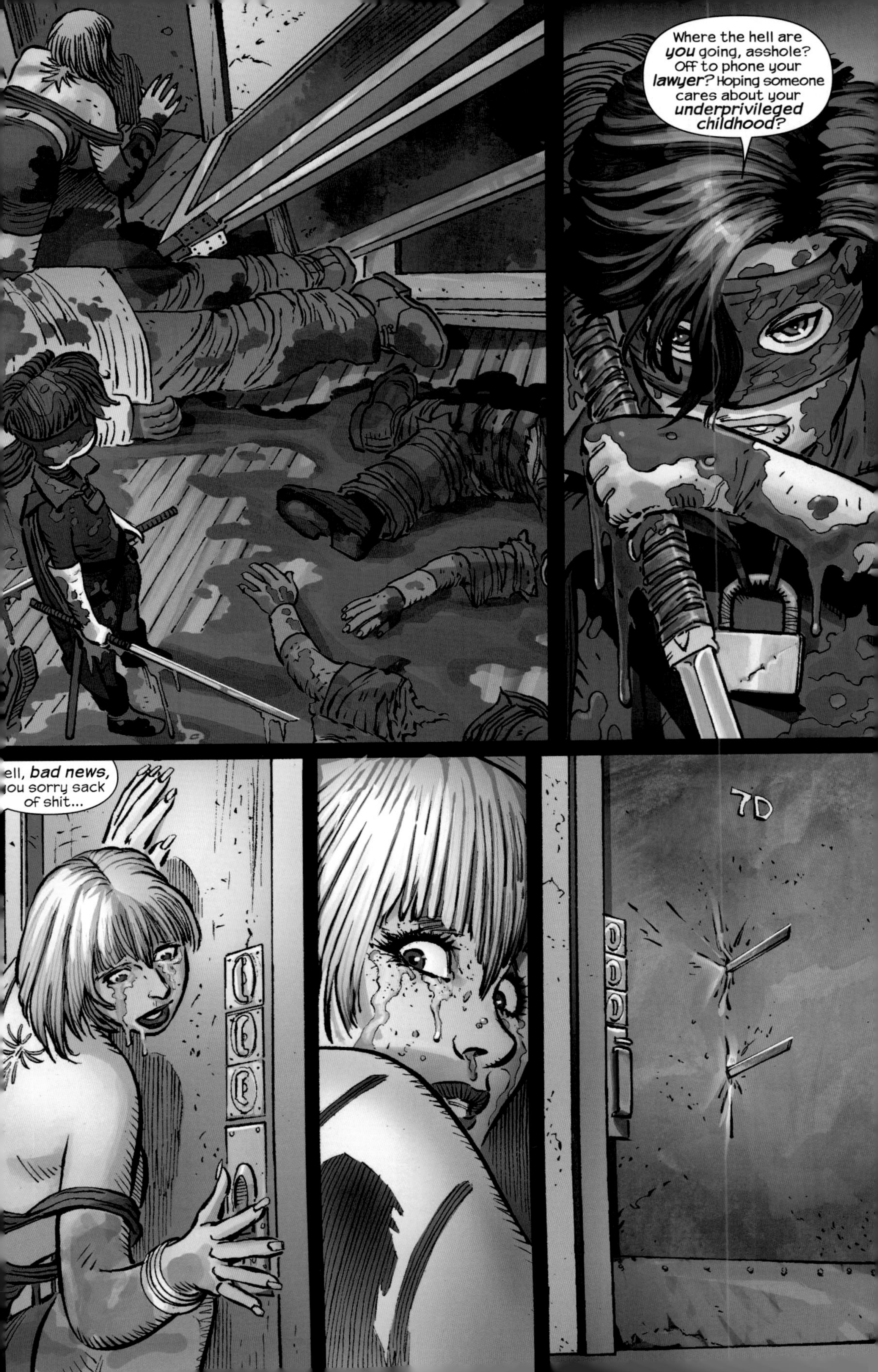
Where the hell are *you* going, asshole? Off to phone your *lawyer*? Hoping someone cares about your *underprivileged childhood*?
ell, *bad news,* ou sorry sack of shit...
7D

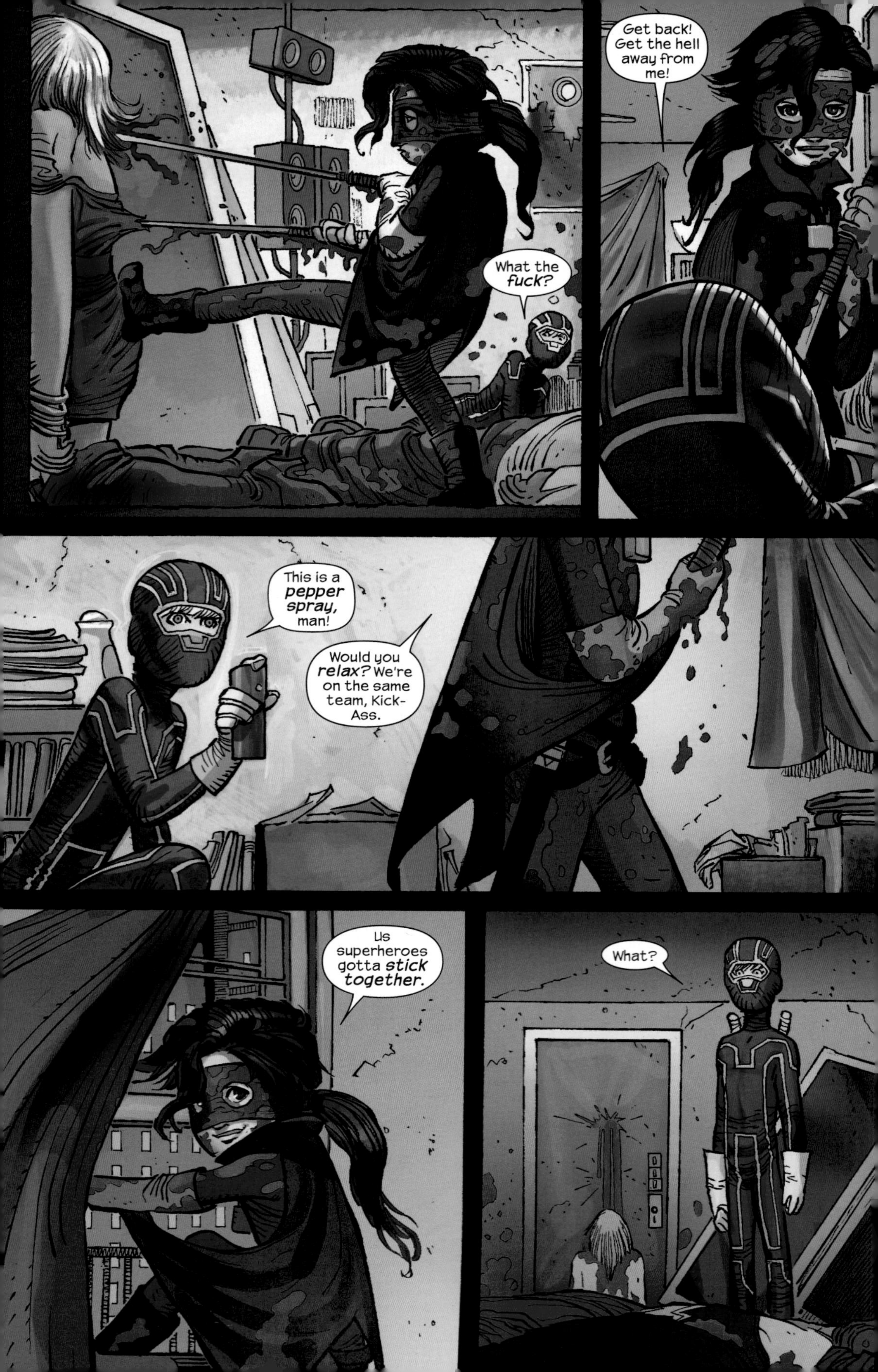
What the fuck?
Get back! Get the hell away from me!
This is a pepper spray, man!
Would you relax? We're on the same team, Kick-Ass.
Us superheroes gotta stick together.
What?

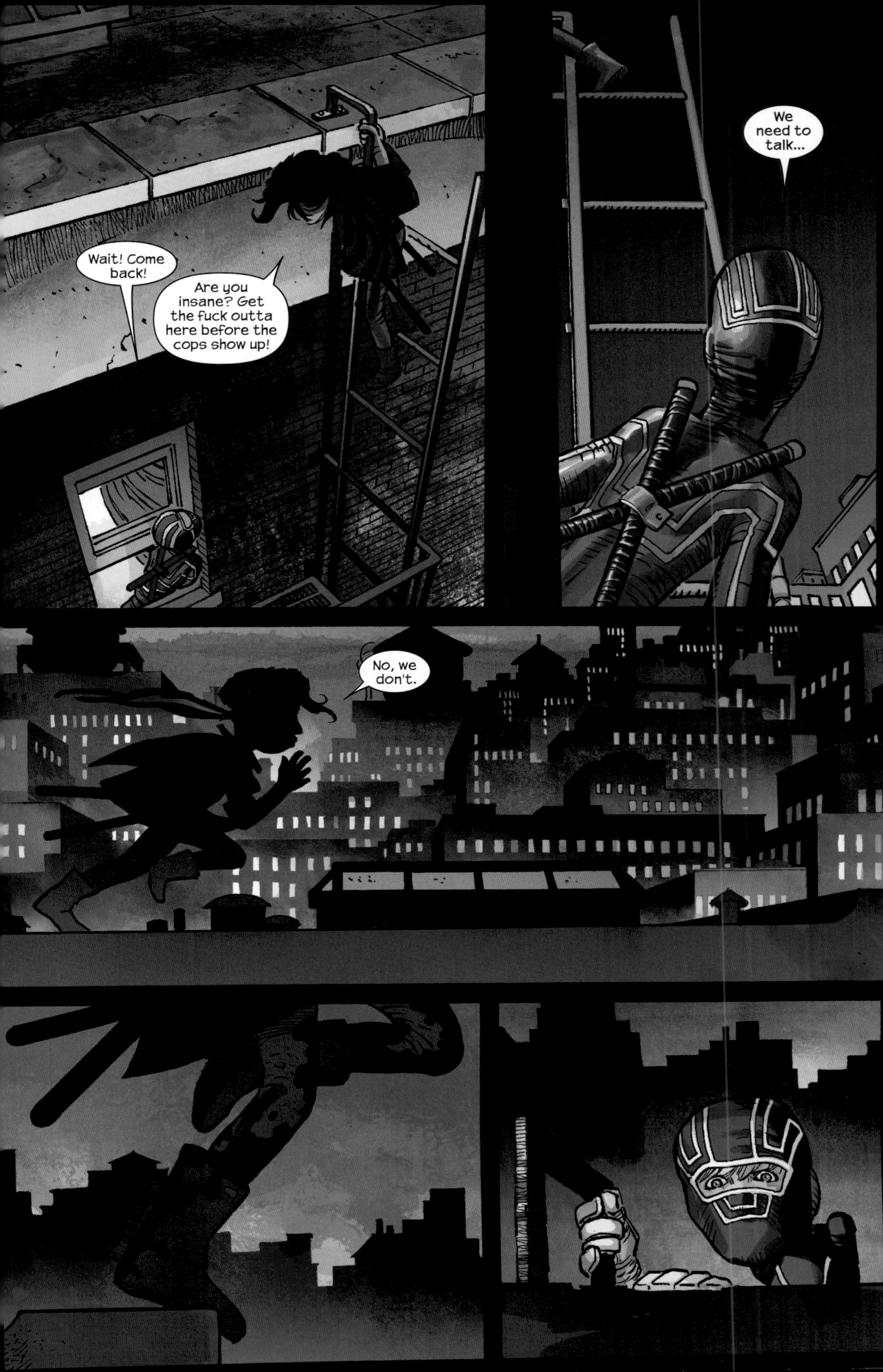
Wait! Come back!
Are you insane? Get the fuck outta here before the cops show up!
We need to talk...
No, we don't.

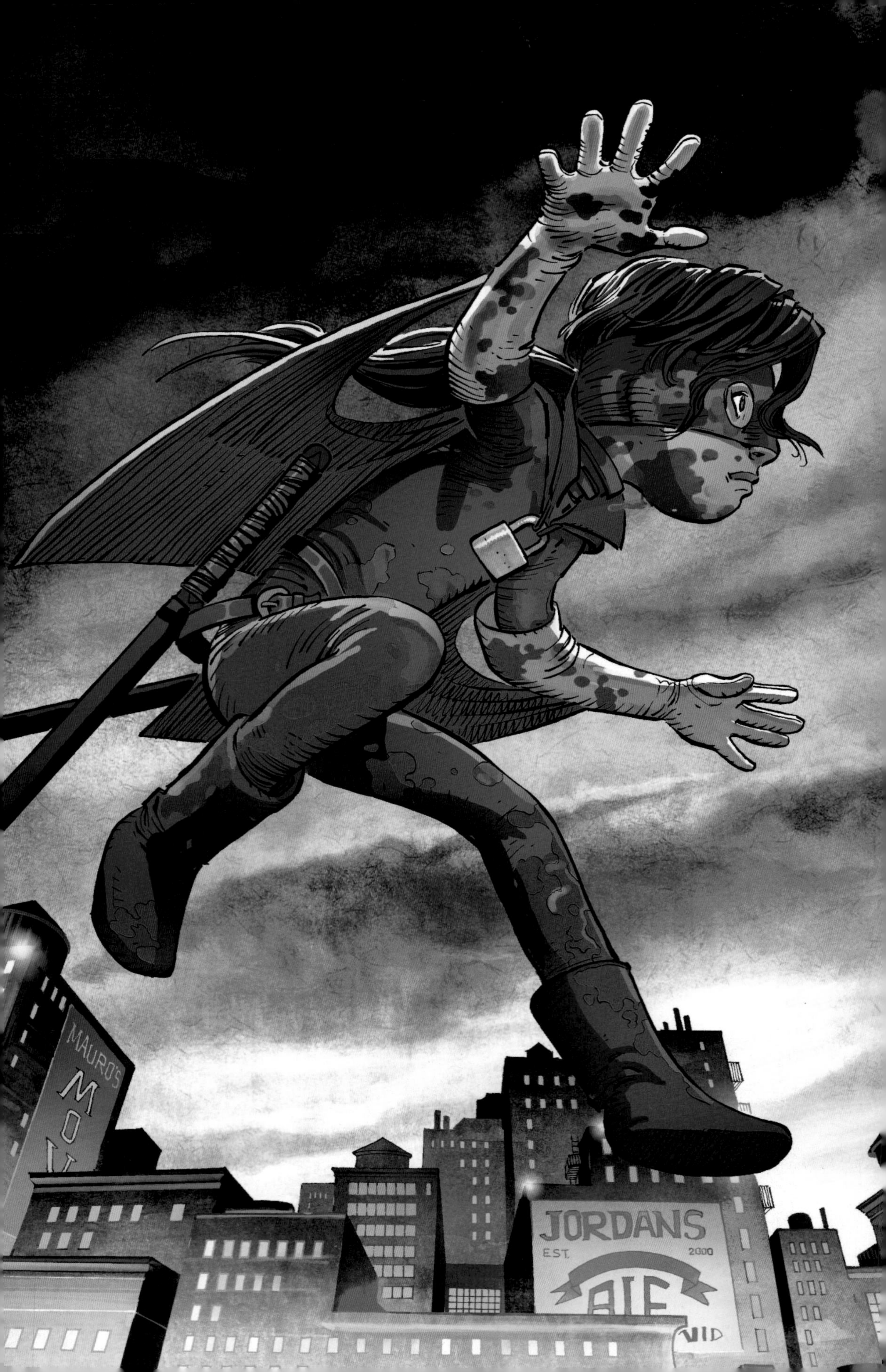
MAURO'S
MOV
JORDANS
EST.
2000
ALE
VID

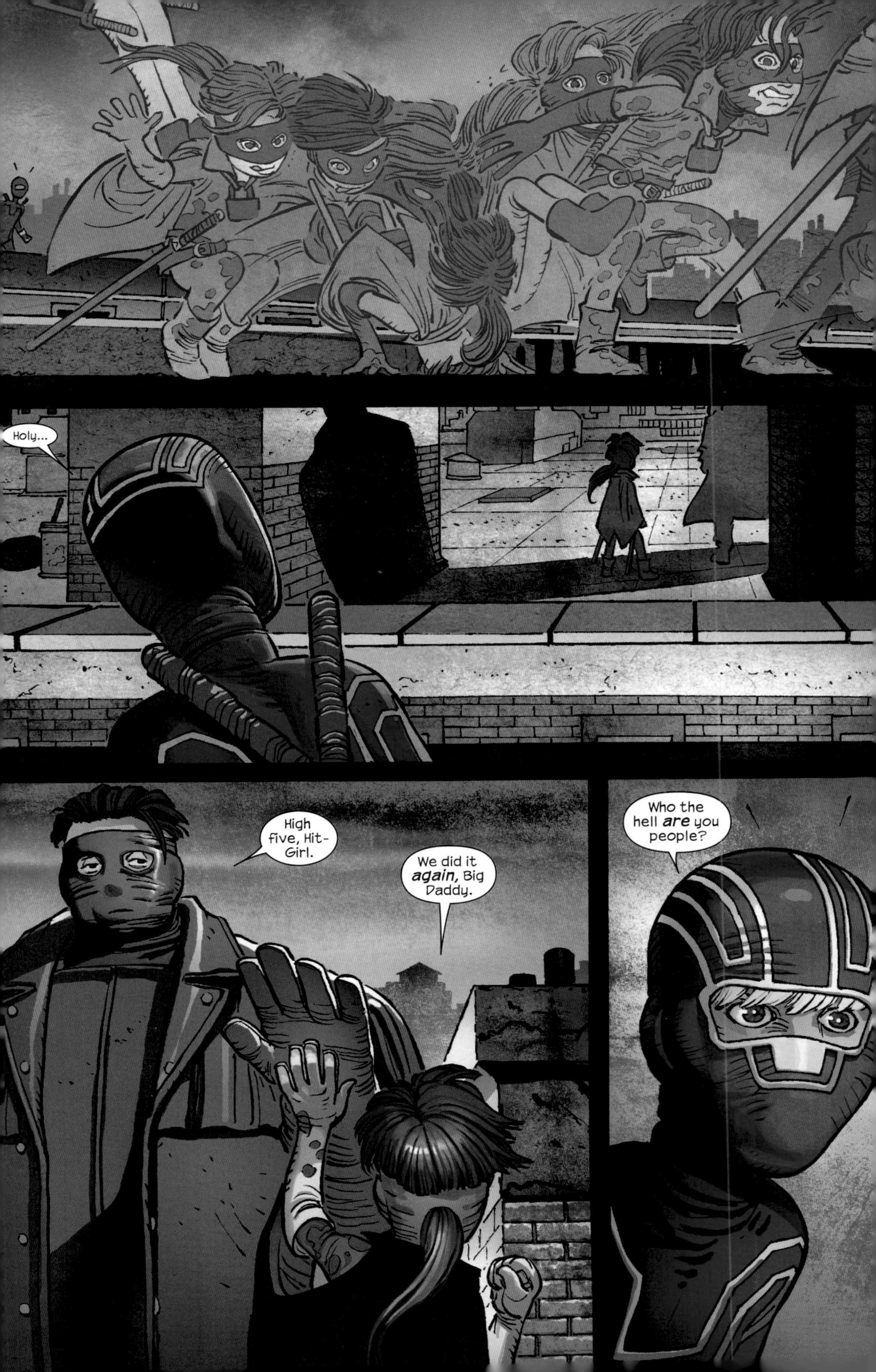
Holy...
High five, Hit-Girl.
We did it *again,* Big Daddy.
Who the hell *are* you people?

Fuck off.

I couldn't believe my *eyes.*

The way they *talked.* The way they *moved.* The way they jumped off buildings without even *blinking.*

These two were *the real deal...*

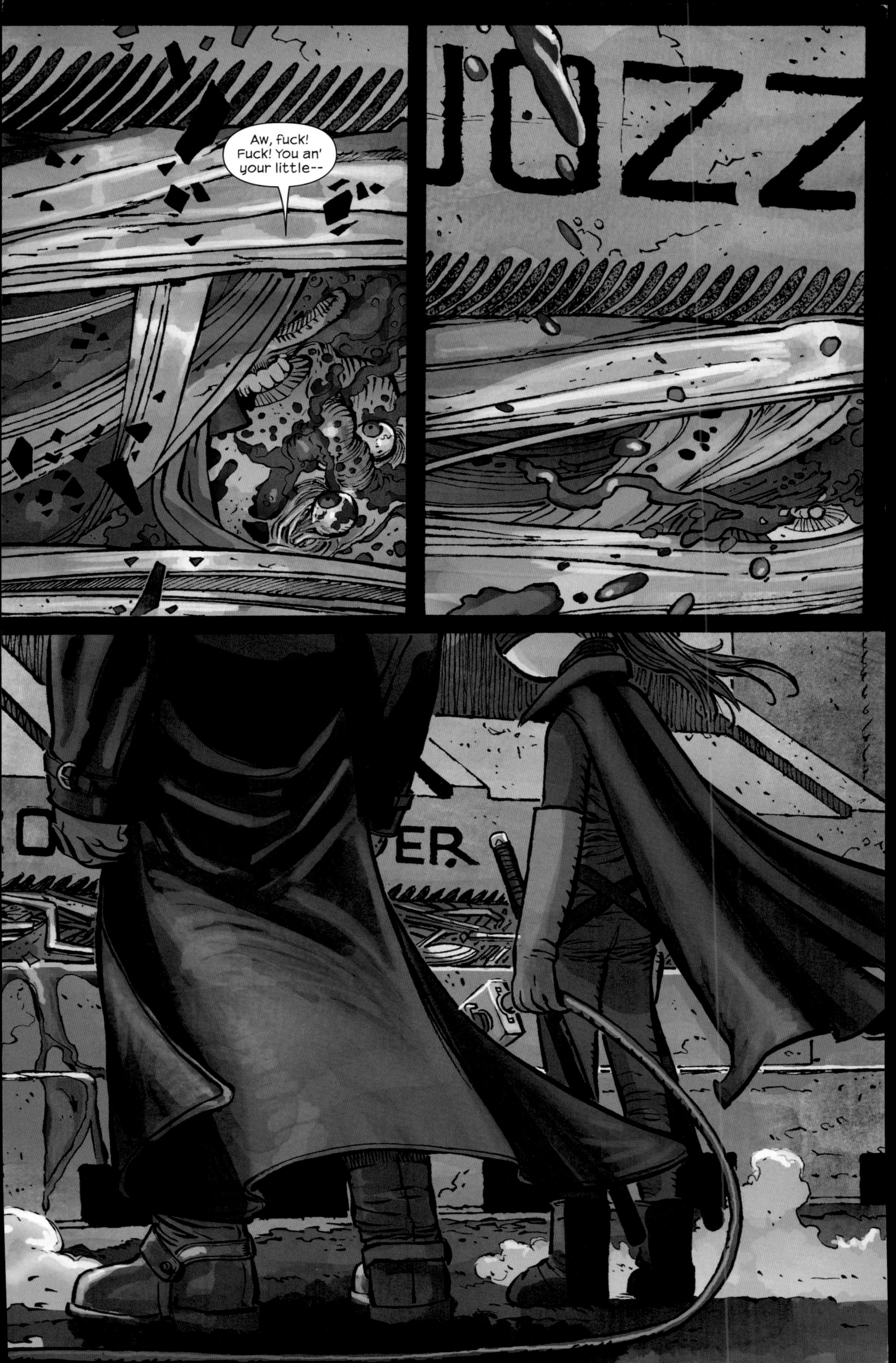
Aw, fuck! Fuck! You an' your little--

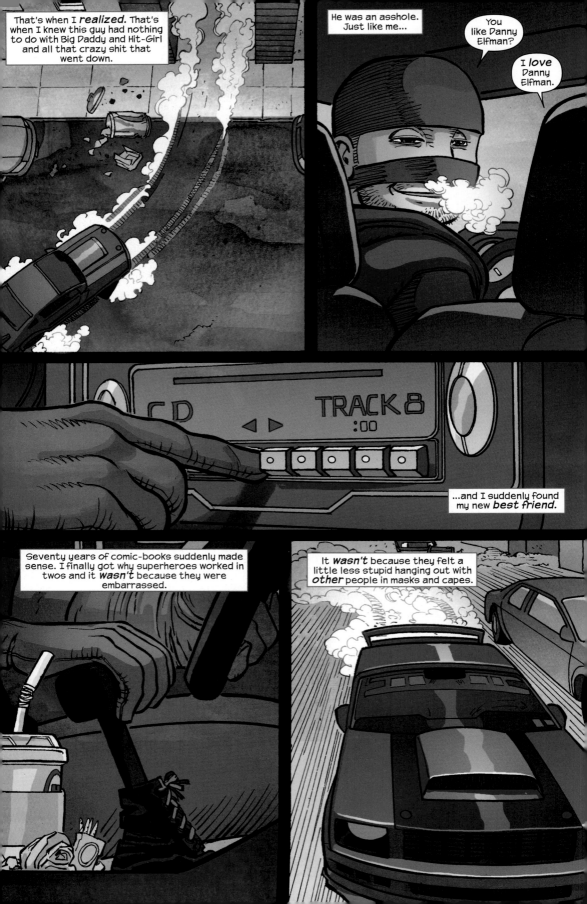

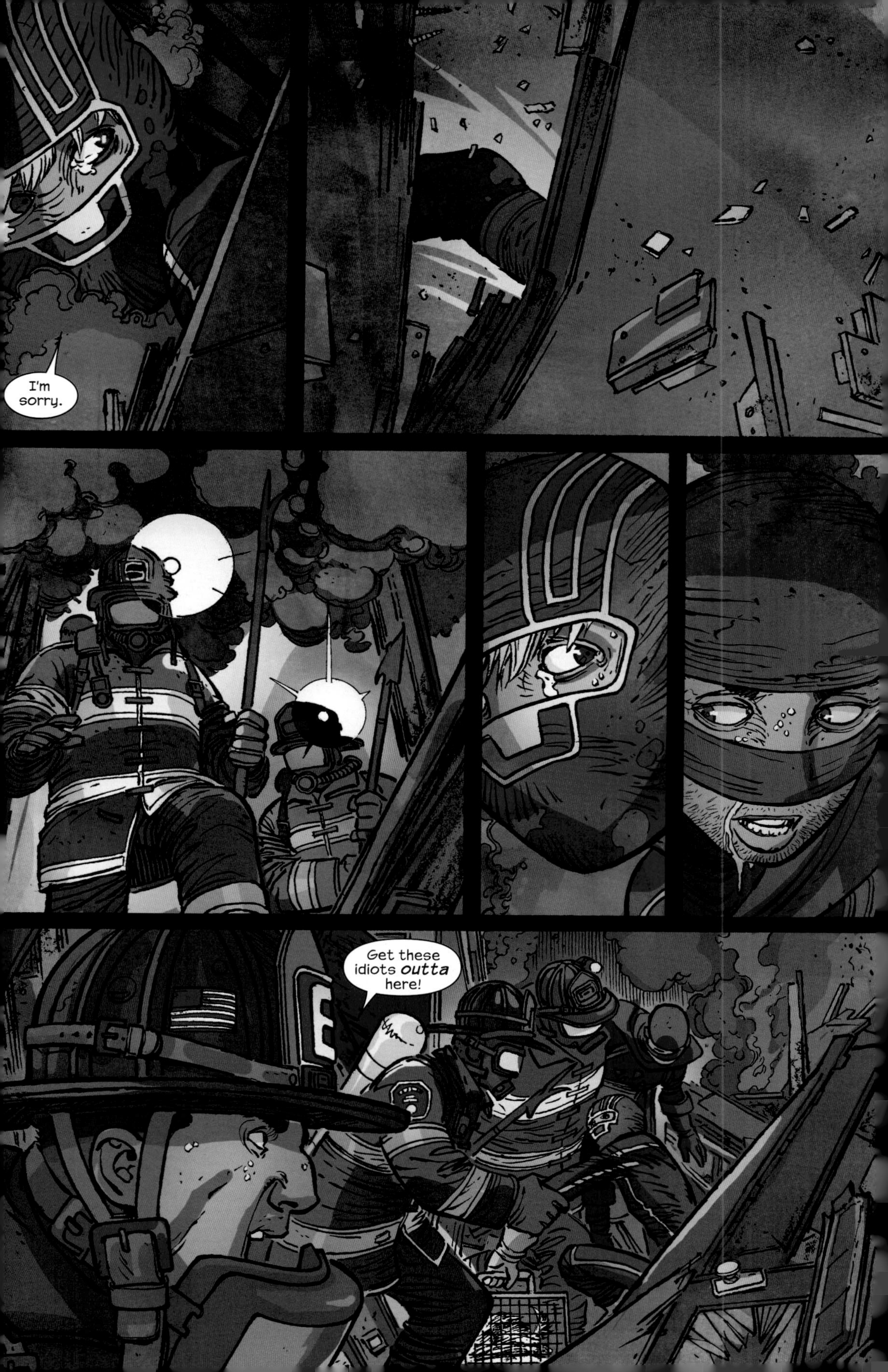
I'm sorry.
Get these idiots *outta* here!

Outside, the crowds went absolutely *nuts*.

Especially when we gave Charlie back to that big, fat crazy lady. The look on her face was a *movie moment*.

This was Superman catching the *helicopter*. Luke destroying the *Death Star*.

Everyone had goosebumps and people were in fucking *tears*.

Of course, we promised the cops we'd *quit* this shit, but it was way too late to get sensible now.

This was superheroes fighting side by side like *Brave and the Bold* or *Marvel Team-Up*.

That meant CNN, NBC, Letterman, Leno and Craig Ferguson.

How the hell could I have even *considered* throwi away the best thing tha ever happened to me?

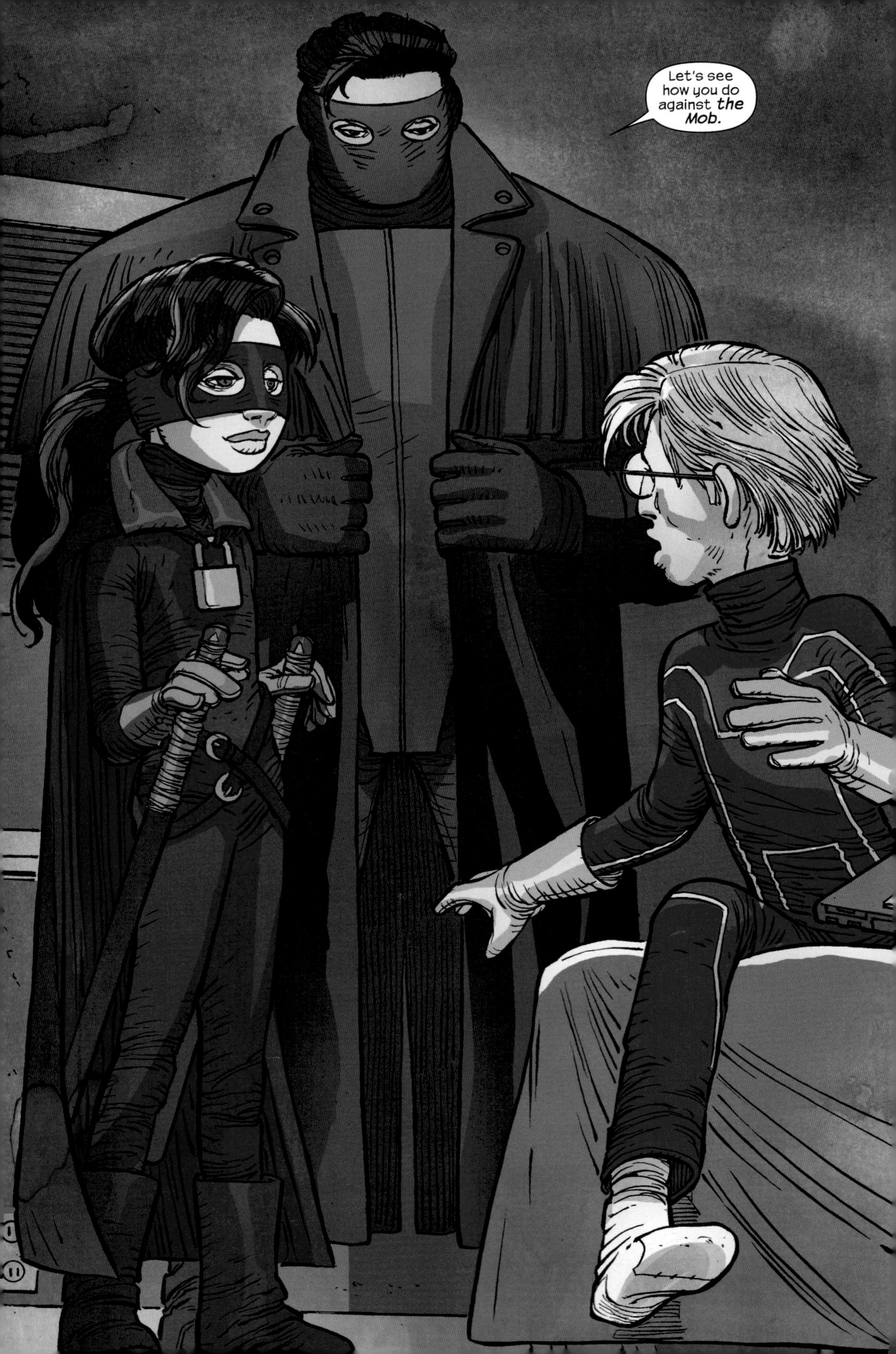
Let's see how you do against *the Mob.*

t-Girl's Diary (age 10 and 1/4):

Daddy, I'm *scared.*

Don't be such a *baby,* Mindy.

Does getting shot *hurt?*

Only for a second. The force of a bullet takes you right off your feet, but it's really no more painful than a punch in the chest.

But I *hate* getting punched in the chest.

You'll be *fine,* sugar-plum.

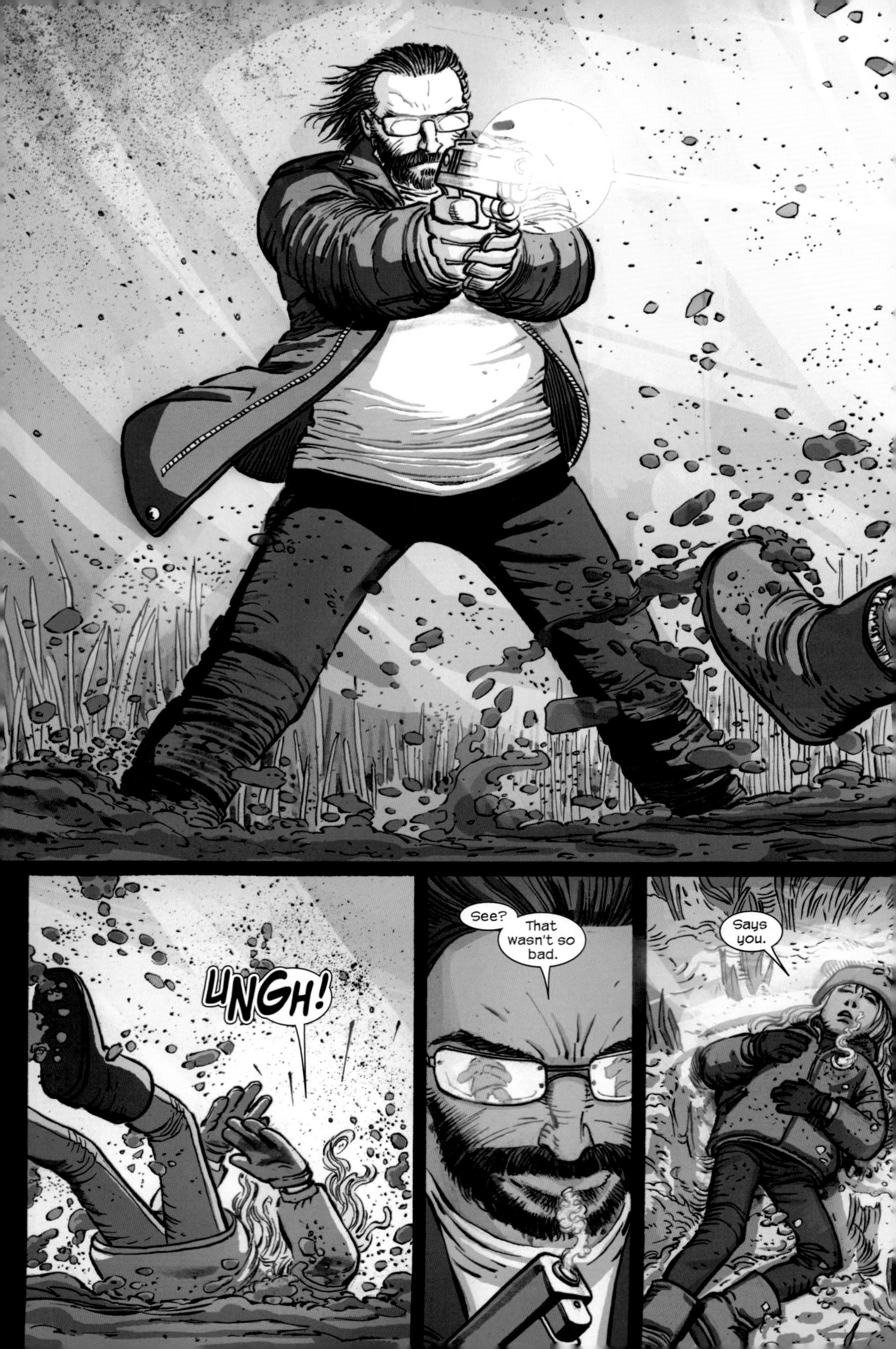
UNGH!
See?
That wasn't so bad.
Says you.

To say my childhood has been unconventional would probably be PRETTY ACCURATE.

Where most girls my age are cooing over Bratz or My Scene dolls, I asked Santa for an M-16 and a pair of silver knuckle-dusters.

Awesome.

WEAPONS FIREARMS

Other girls beg for new pair of HEELIE I'm begging Dad for PEARL-HANDLED SWITCHBLADE.

Oo. I like *that* one, Daddy.

We eat lamb's heart for breakfast, chops for lunch and a big plate of liver for dinner every night.

KISS MY COP

I don't need toys. I don't need friends. I don't need school...

HIT IT, BABY! HIT THIS BAG OF SHIT LIKE IT'S MICHAEL FUCKING MOORE!

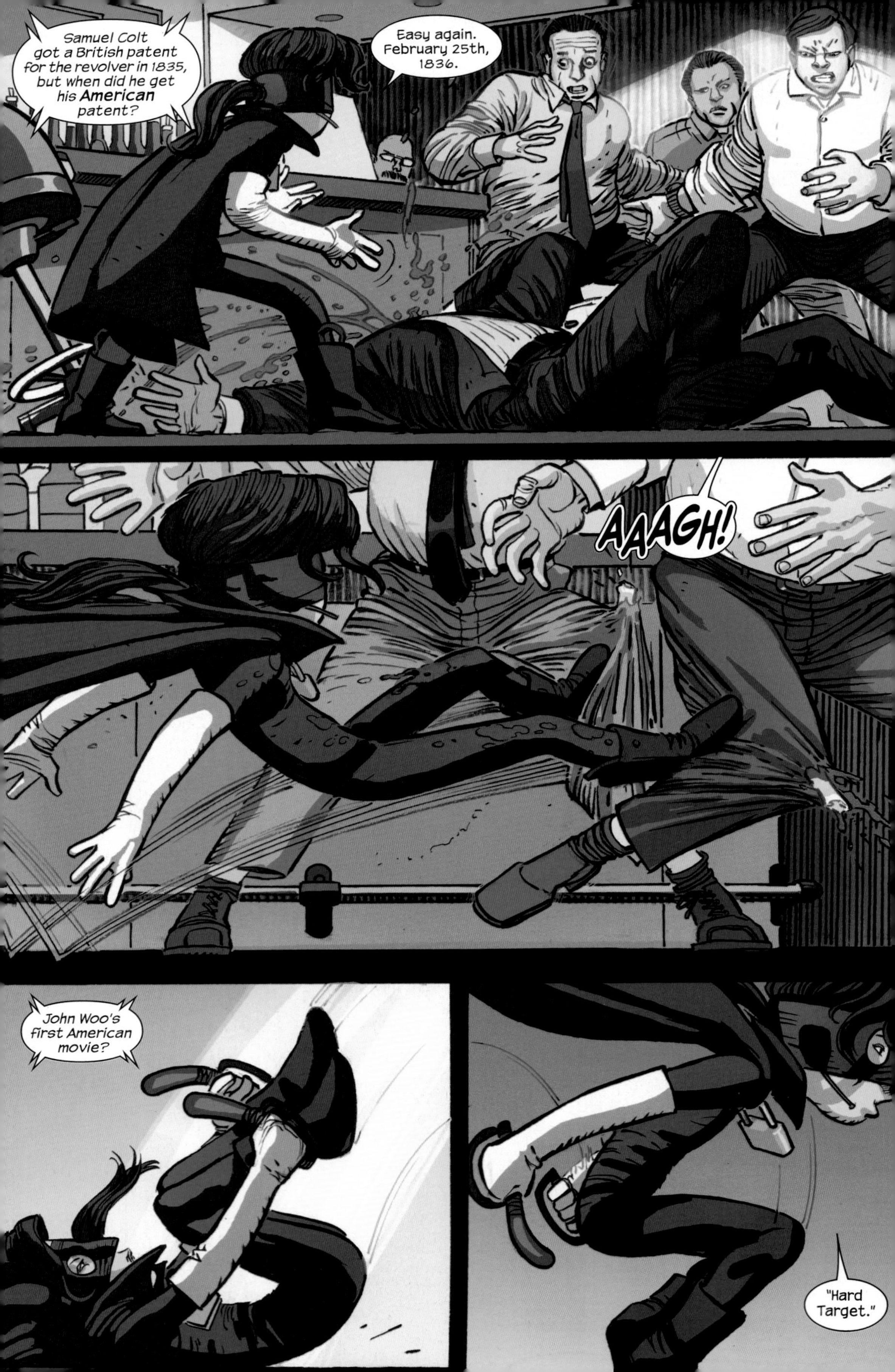
Samuel Colt got a British patent for the revolver in 1835, but when did he get his **American** patent?
Easy again. February 25th, 1836.
AAAGH!
John Woo's first American movie?
"Hard Target."

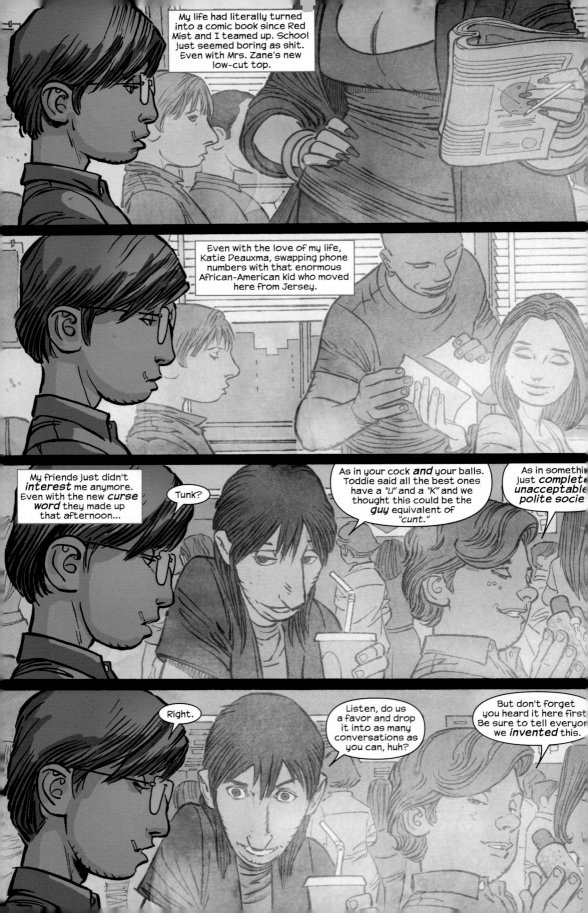

My life had literally turned into a comic book since Red Mist and I teamed up. School just seemed boring as shit. Even with Mrs. Zane's new low-cut top.

Even with the love of my life, Katie Deauxma, swapping phone numbers with that enormous African-American kid who moved here from Jersey.

My friends just didn't *interest* me anymore. Even with the new *curse word* they made up that afternoon...

Tunk?

As in your cock *and* your balls. Toddie said all the best ones have a "U" and a "K" and we thought this could be the *guy* equivalent of "cunt."

As in somethi just *complet* unacceptable polite socie

Right.

Listen, do us a favor and drop it into as many conversations as you can, huh?

But don't forget you heard it here first Be sure to tell everyor we *invented* this.

Let's just **talk** to them and see if we can work this out, okay?

Sure.

I don't know if it was contact-high from Red Mist's weed or if I was just **stressed out**. But there was **no way** I was getting any sleep that night.

I paced the streets for hours and hours, running through all the cool stuff I'd say when we finally had our face-off.

Would they kill us like they killed Eddie Lomas?

Nah, just because they were hardcore didn't mean they were Doctor Doom. Even the **biggest** badasses follow some kind of **superhero code**

Hey, *shithead!*

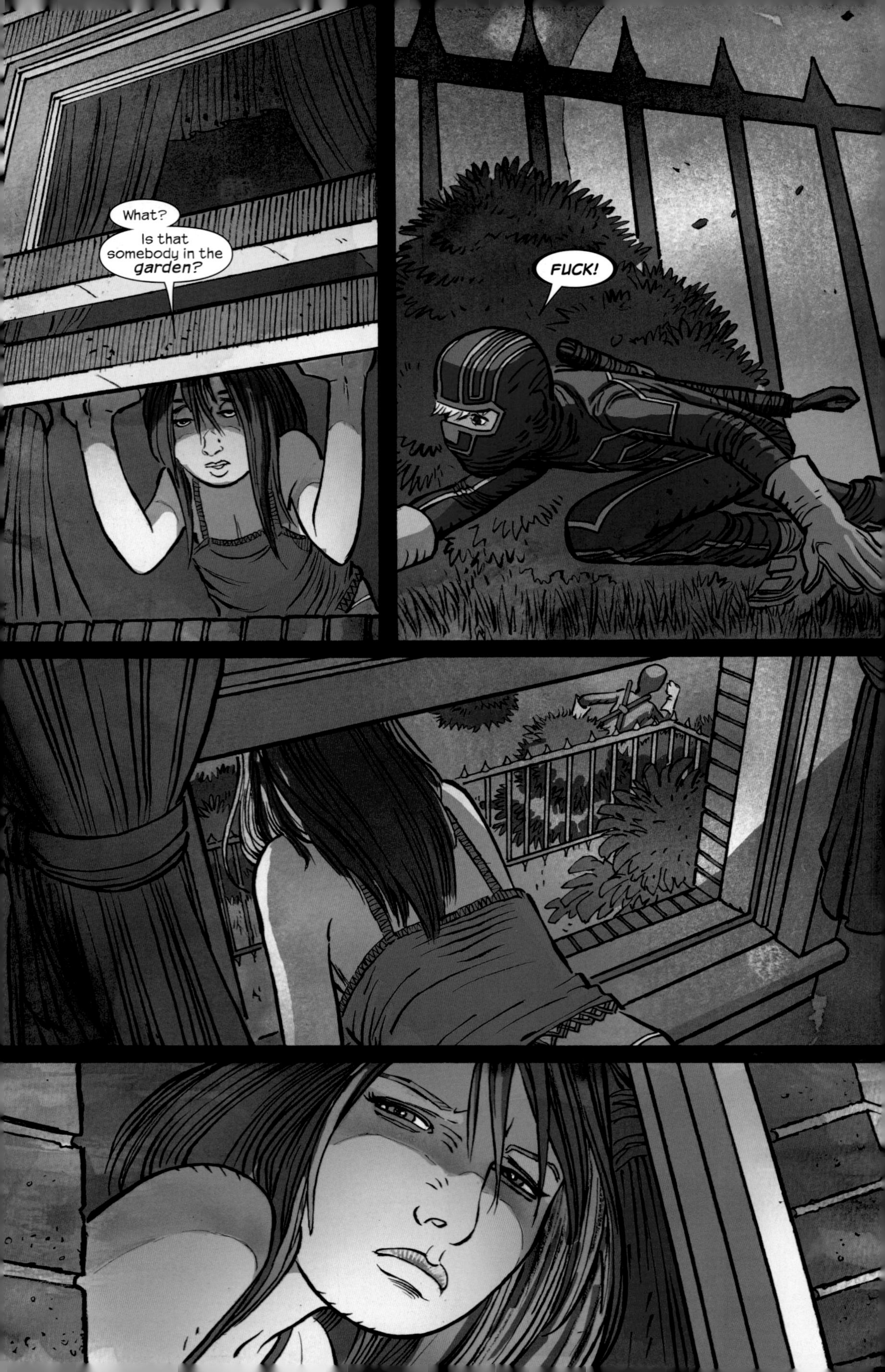
What?
Is that somebody in the *garden*?
FUCK!

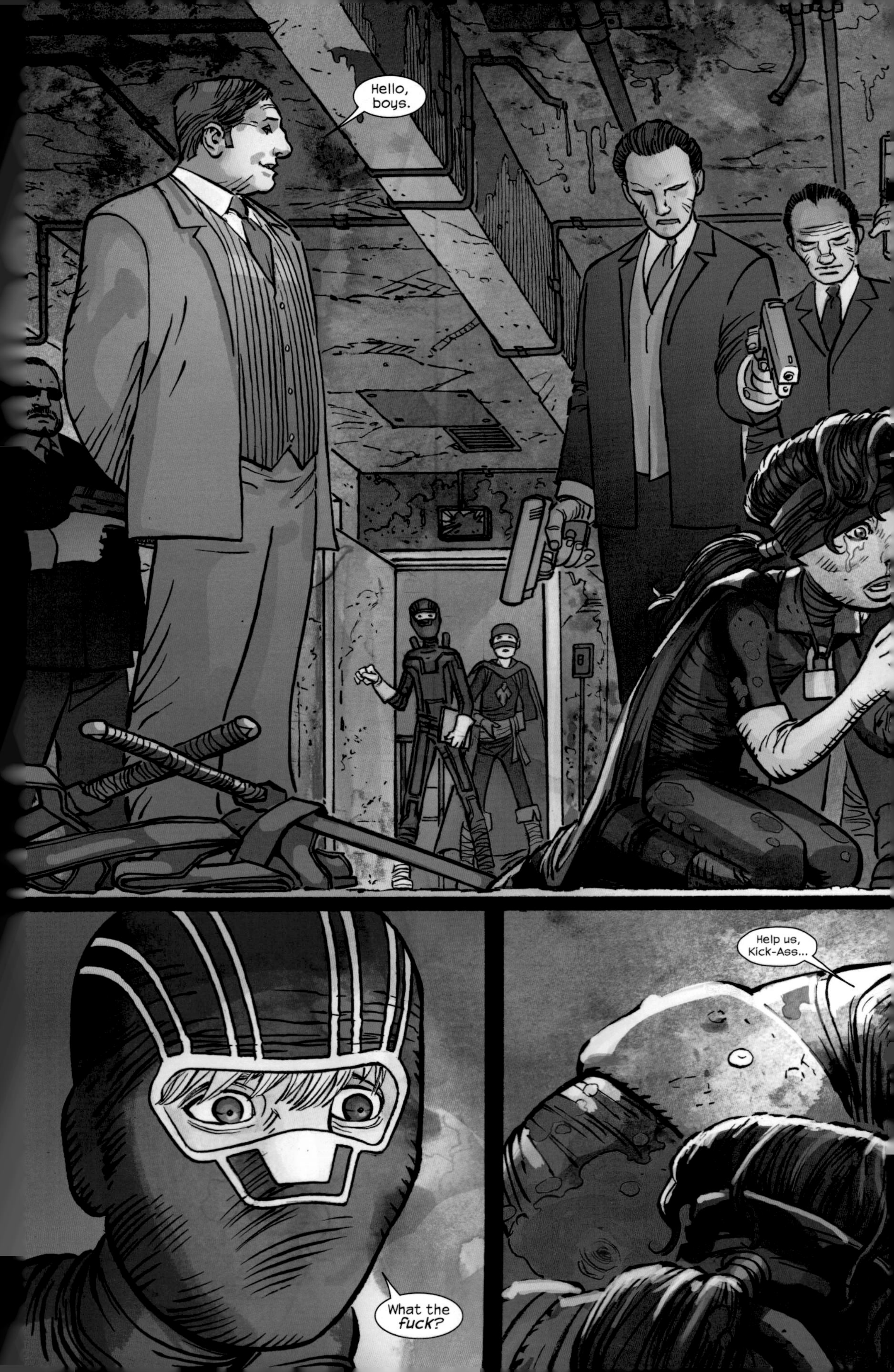
Hello, boys.
What the *fuck?*
Help us, Kick-Ass...

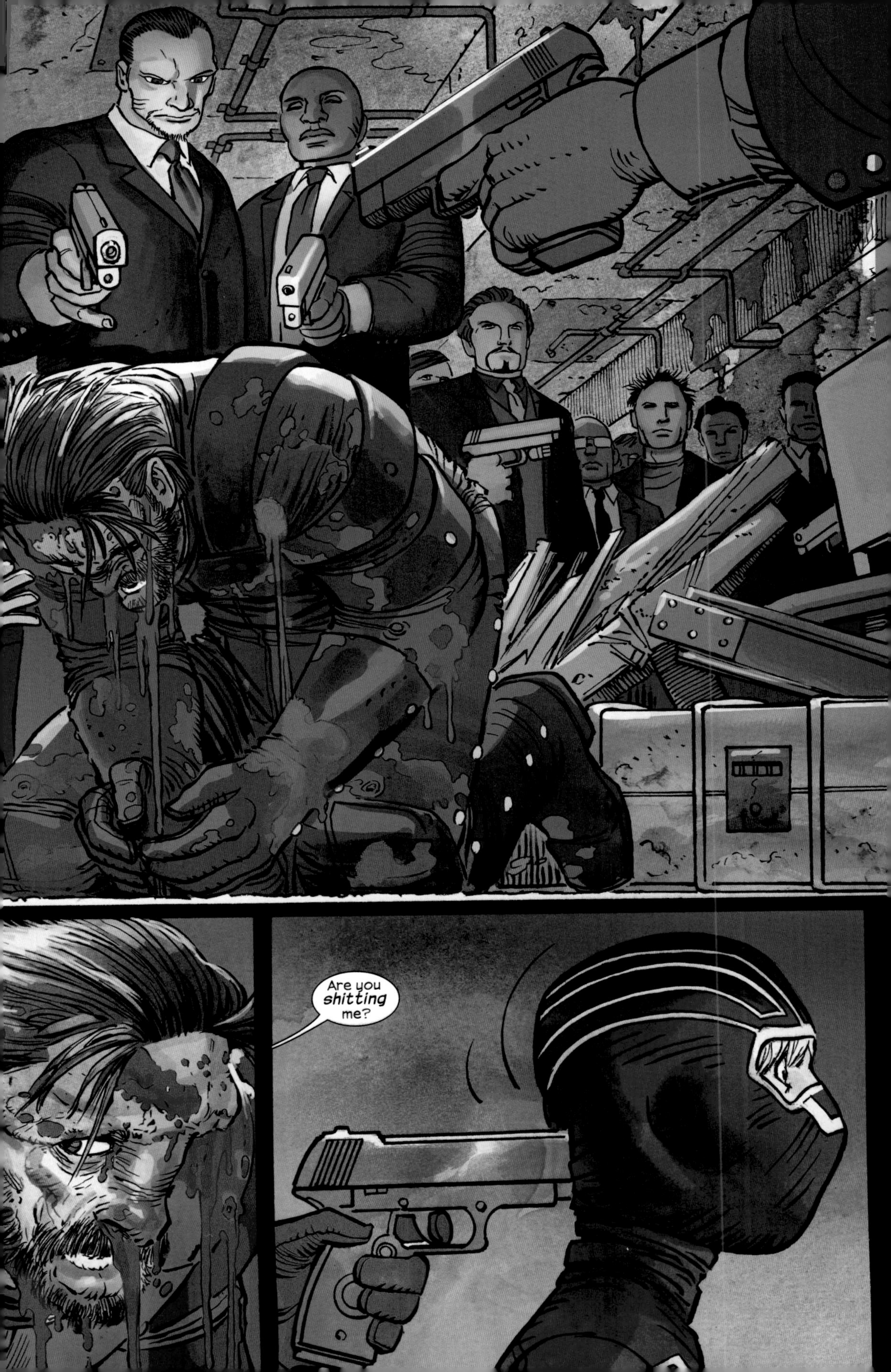
Are you shitting me?

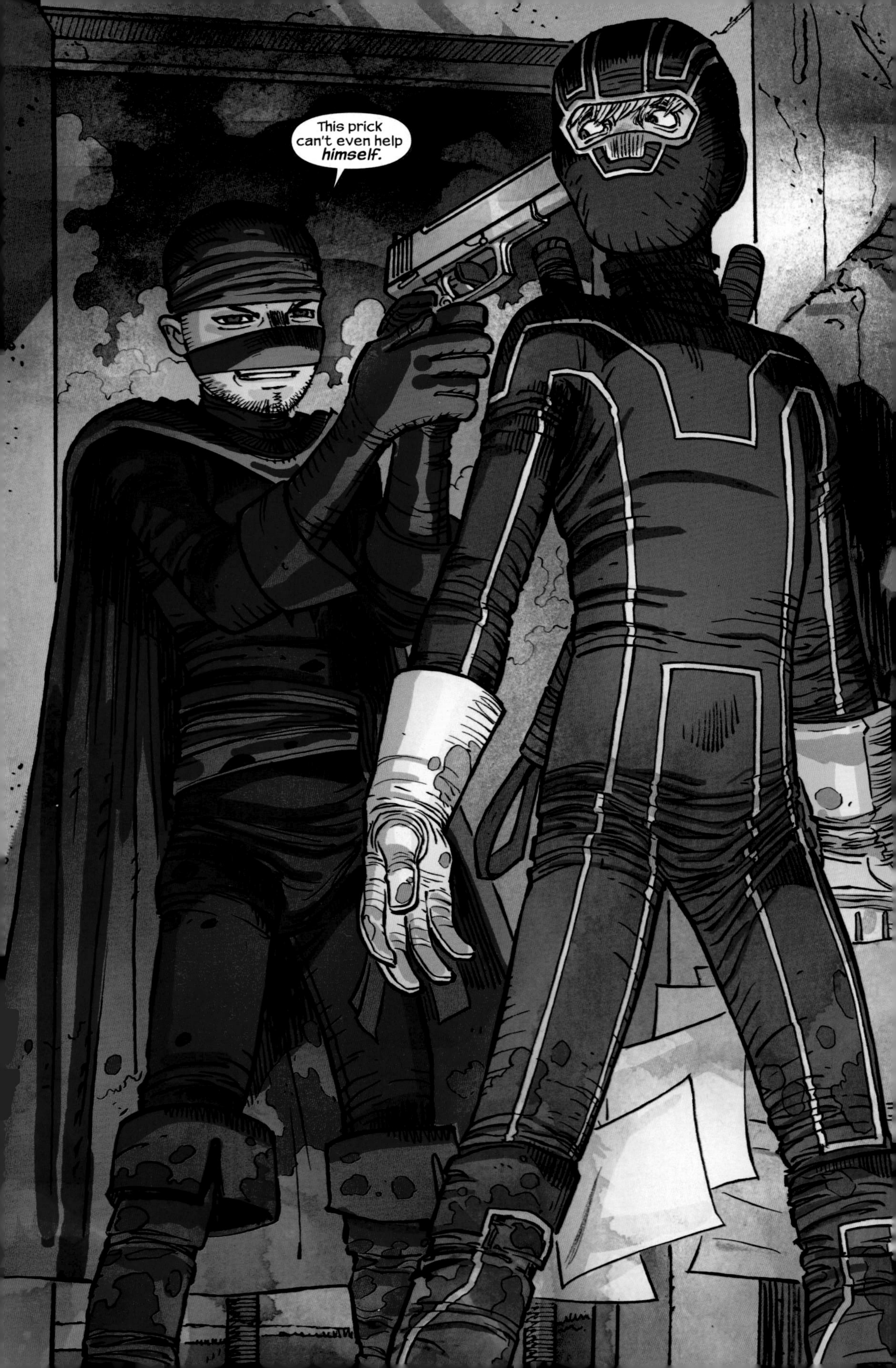
This prick can't even help *himself.*

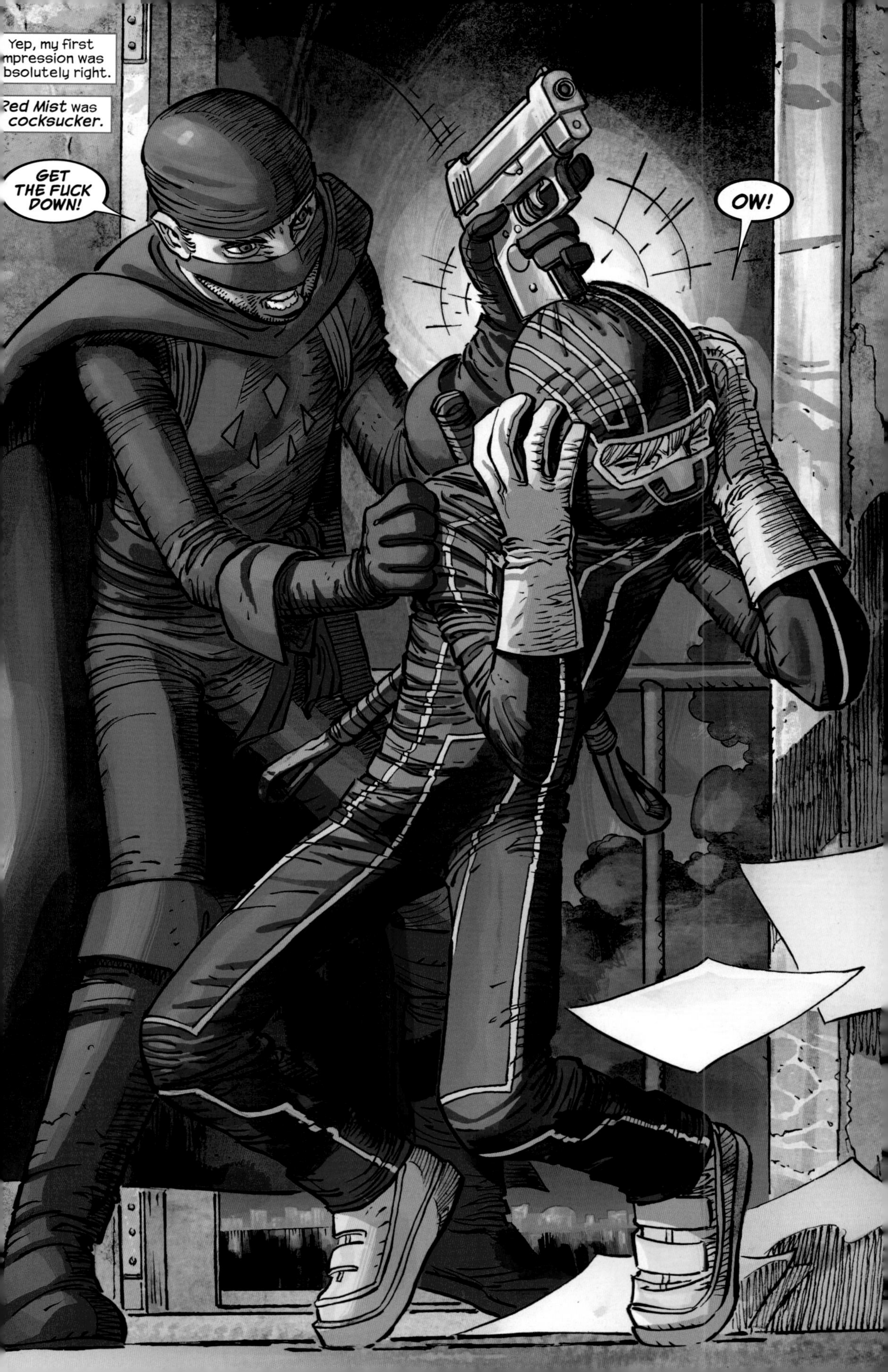
Yep, my first
mpression was
bsolutely right.
Red Mist was
cocksucker.
GET THE FUCK DOWN!
OW!

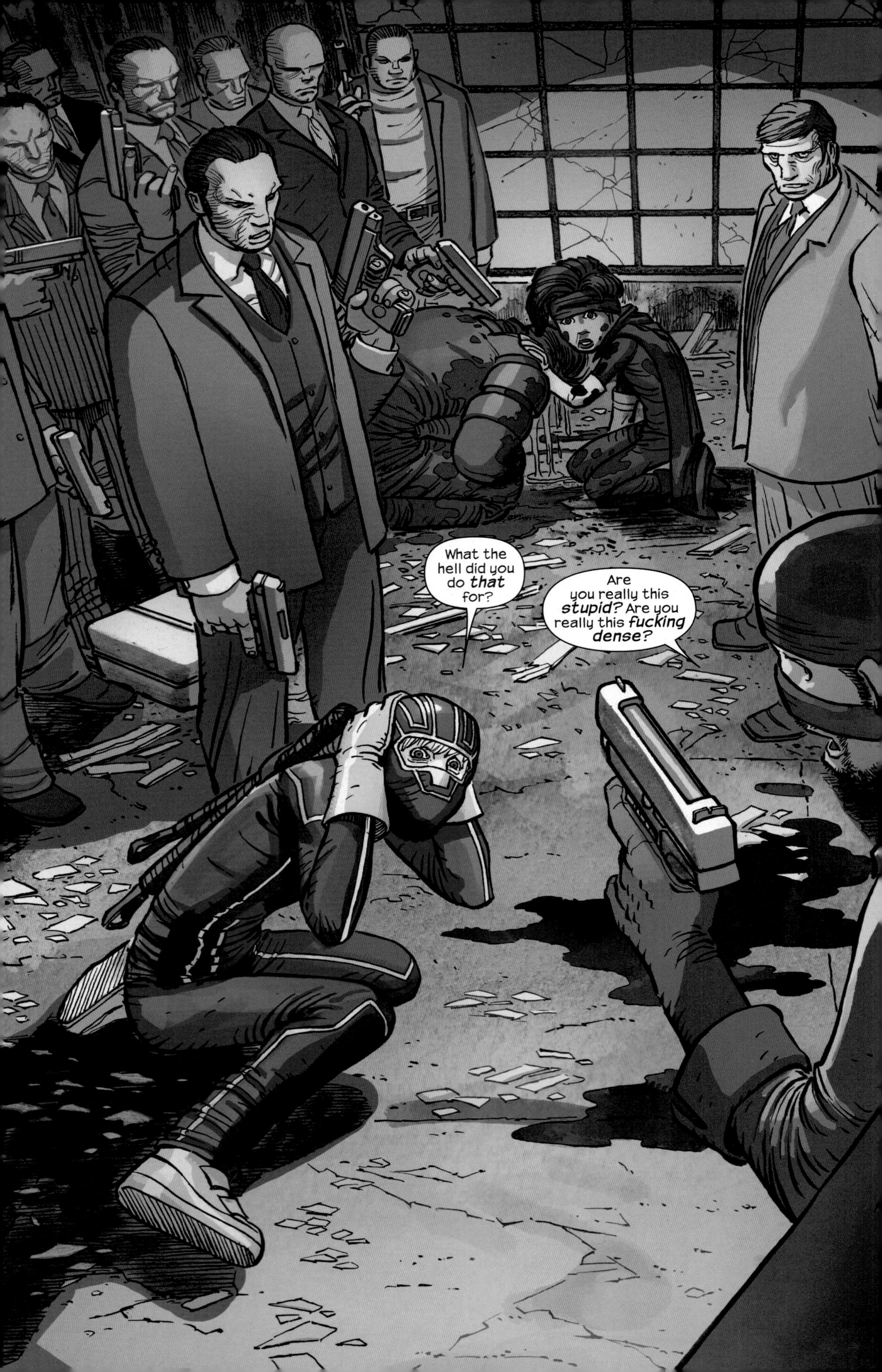
What the hell did you do *that* for?
Are you really this *stupid?* Are you really this *fucking dense?*

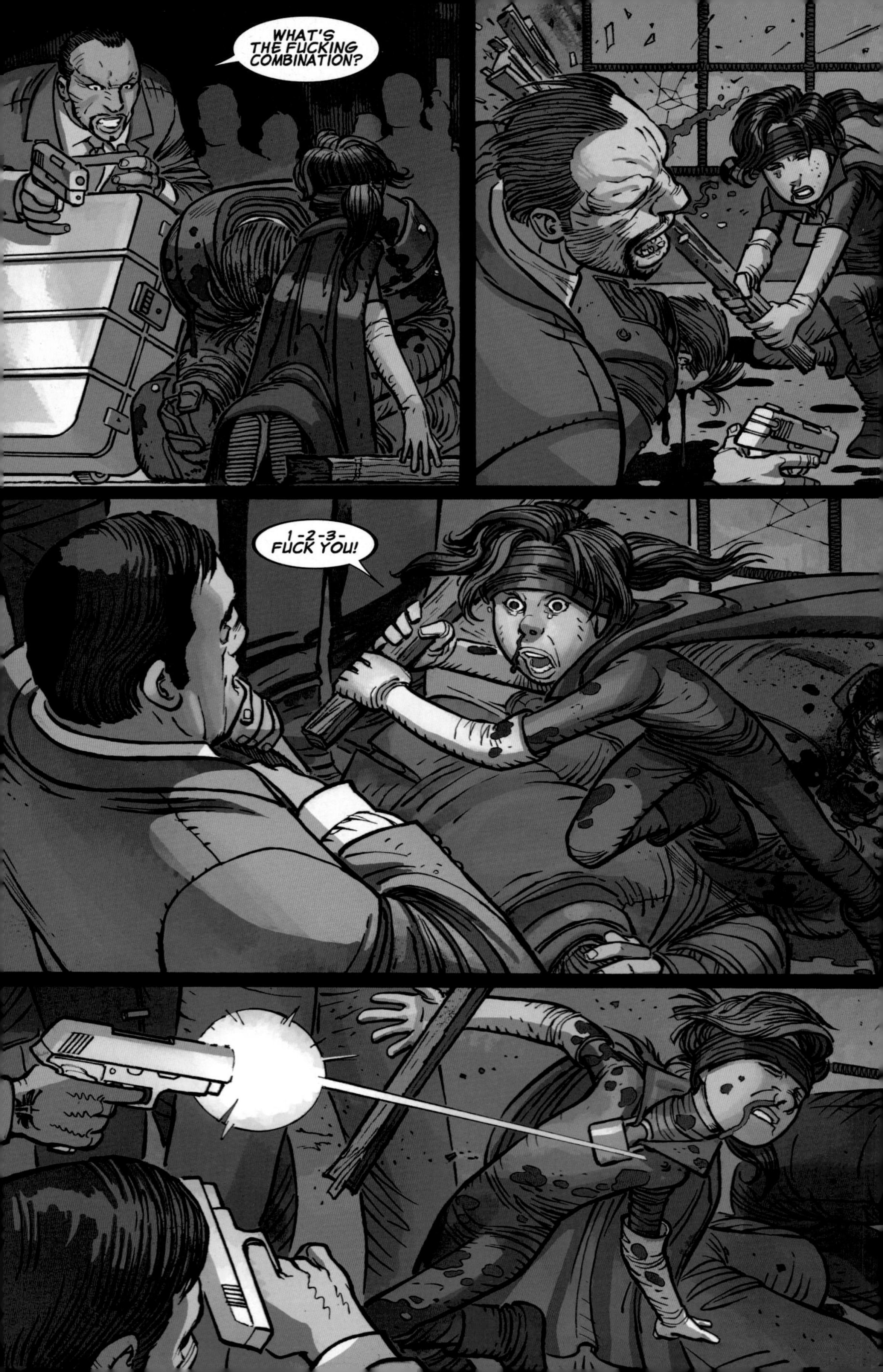
WHAT'S THE FUCKING COMBINATION?
1-2-3- FUCK YOU!

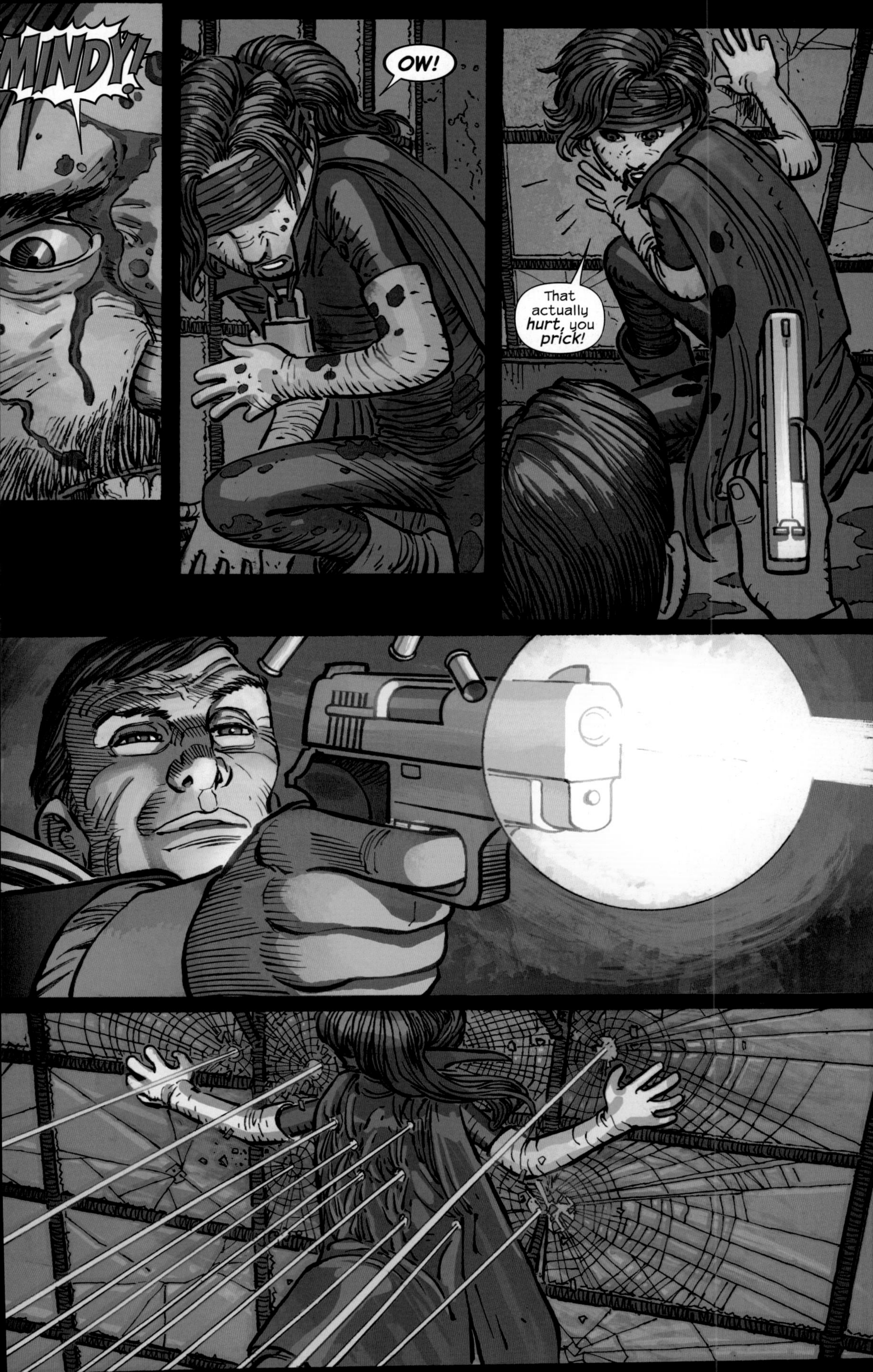
MINDY!
OW!
That actually hurt, you prick!

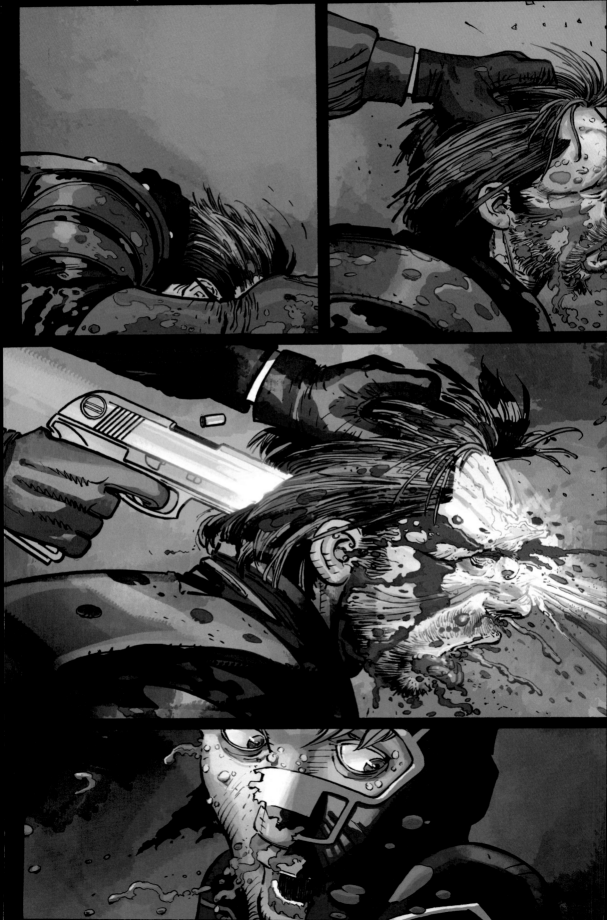

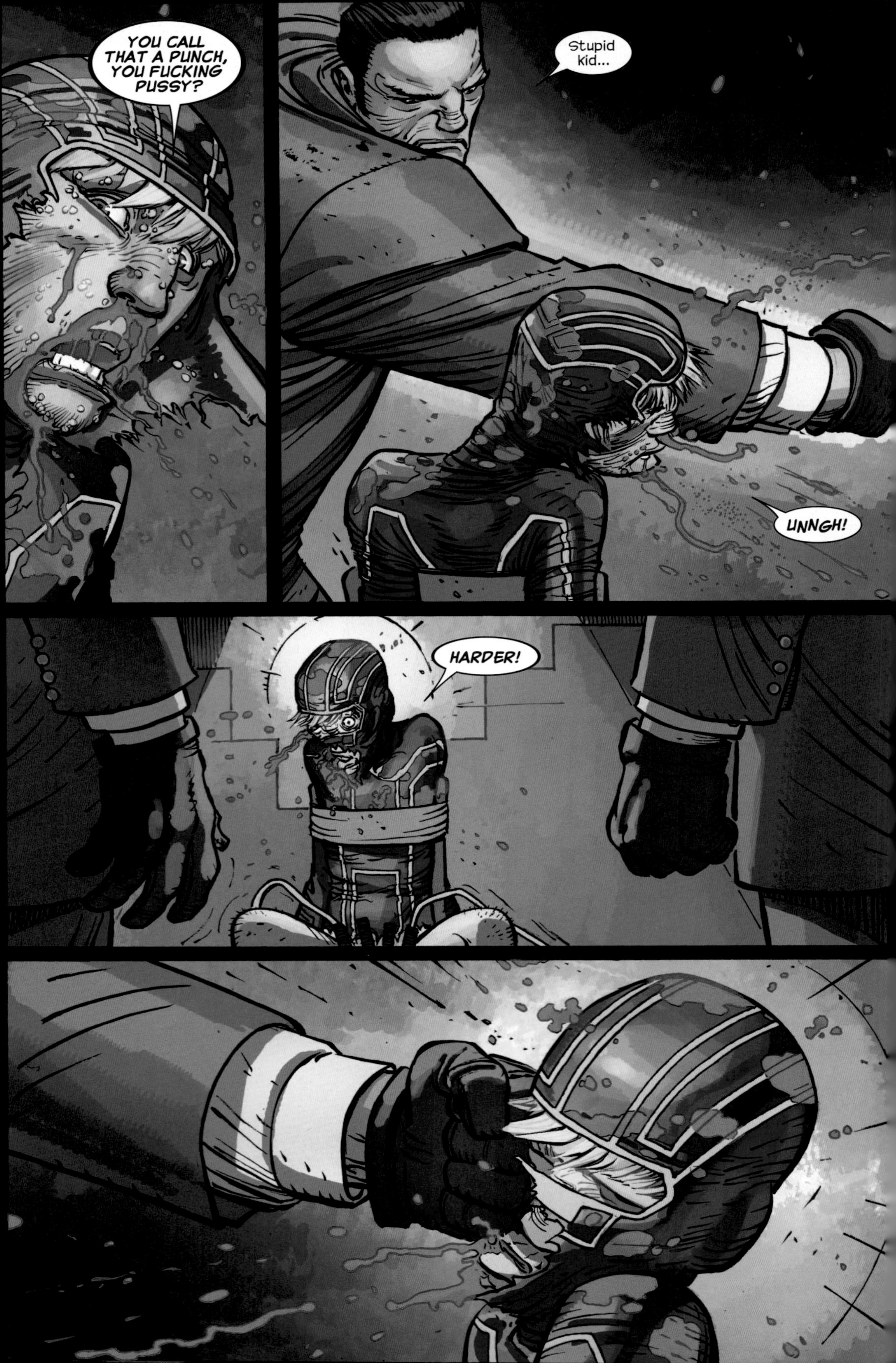
YOU CALL THAT A PUNCH, YOU FUCKING PUSSY?
Stupid kid...
UNNGH!
HARDER!

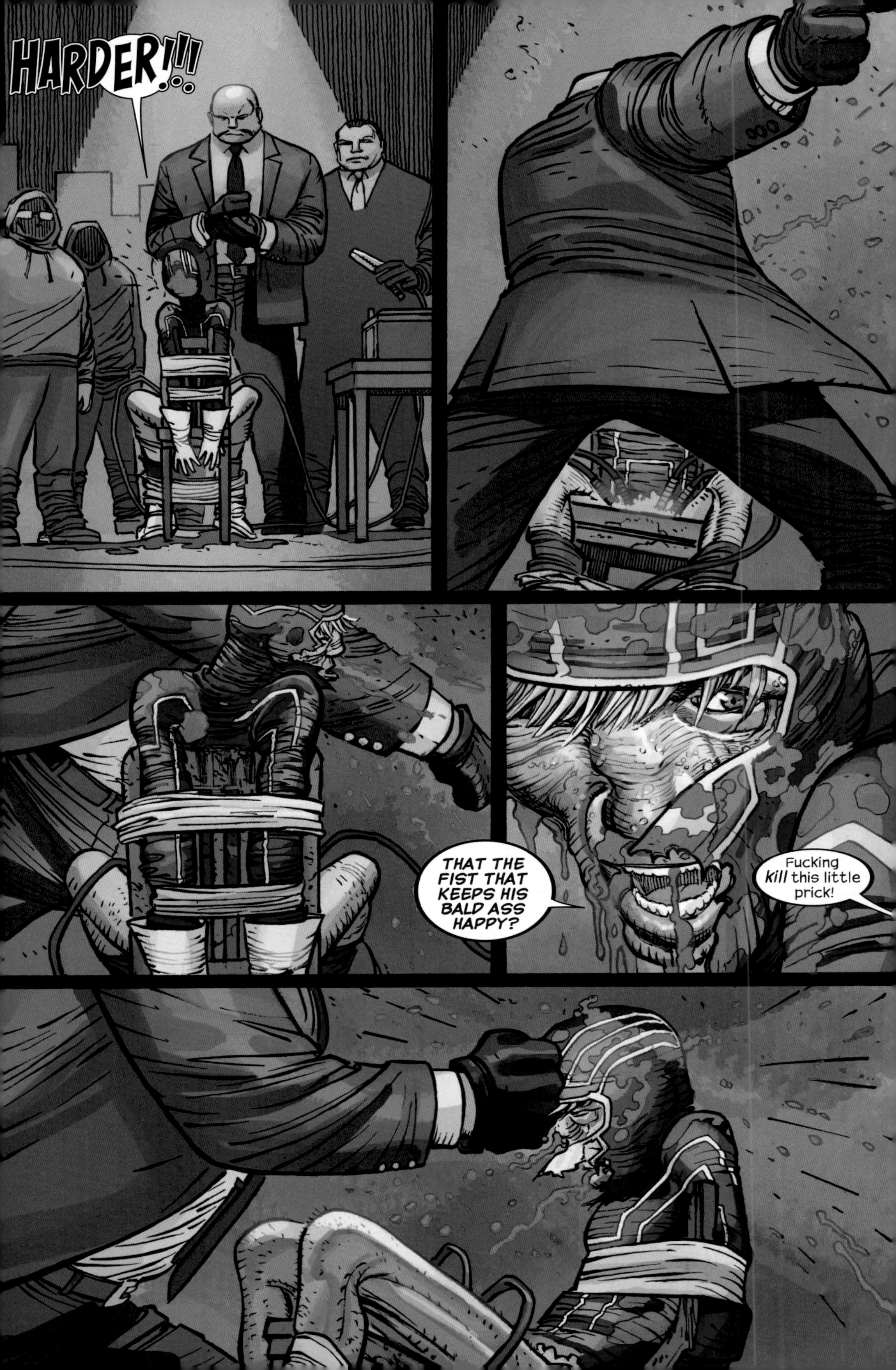
HARDER!!!
THAT THE FIST THAT KEEPS HIS BALD ASS HAPPY?
Fucking *kill* this little prick!

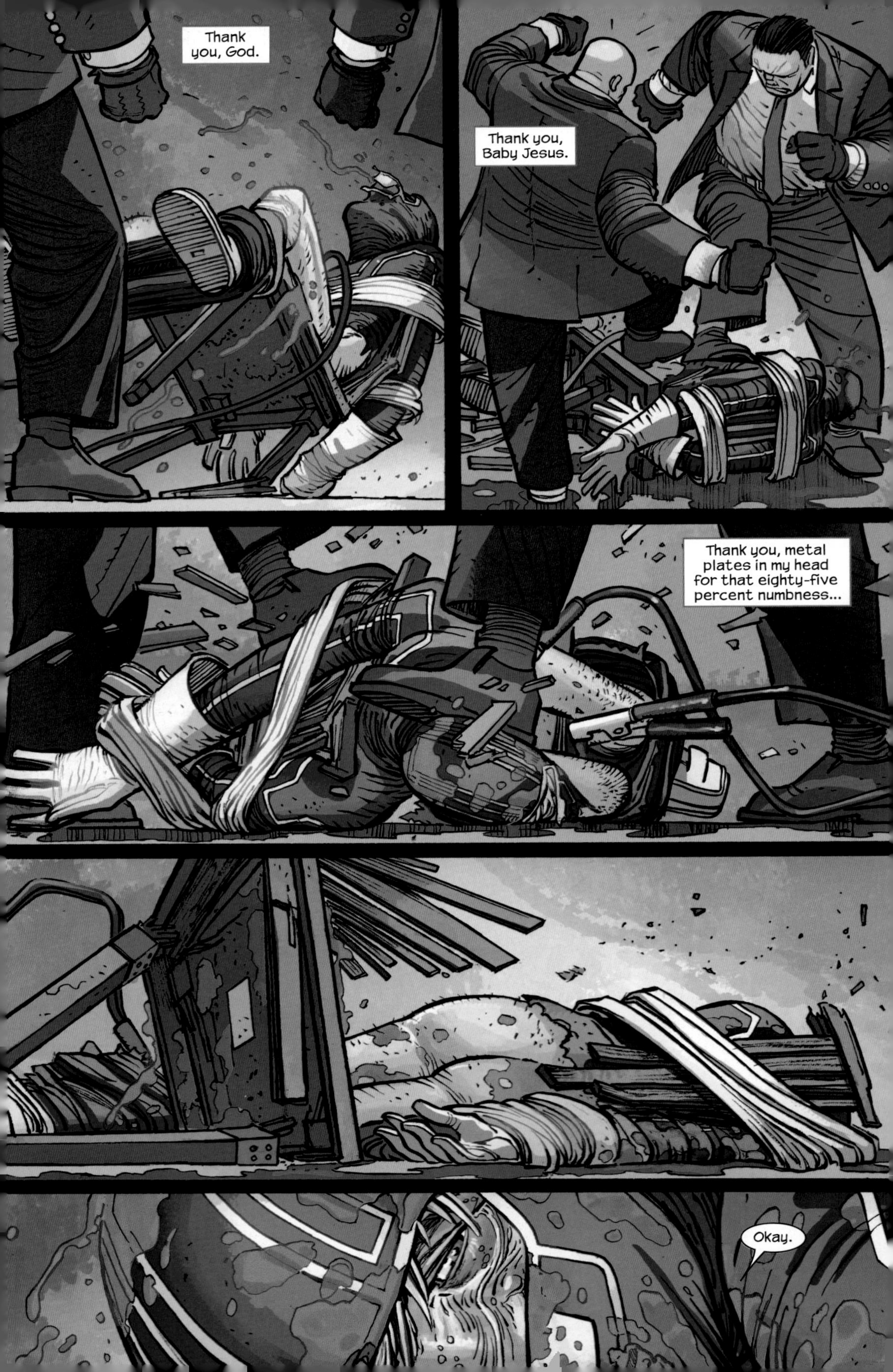

Thank you, God.
Thank you, Baby Jesus.
Thank you, metal plates in my head for that eighty-five percent numbness...
Okay.

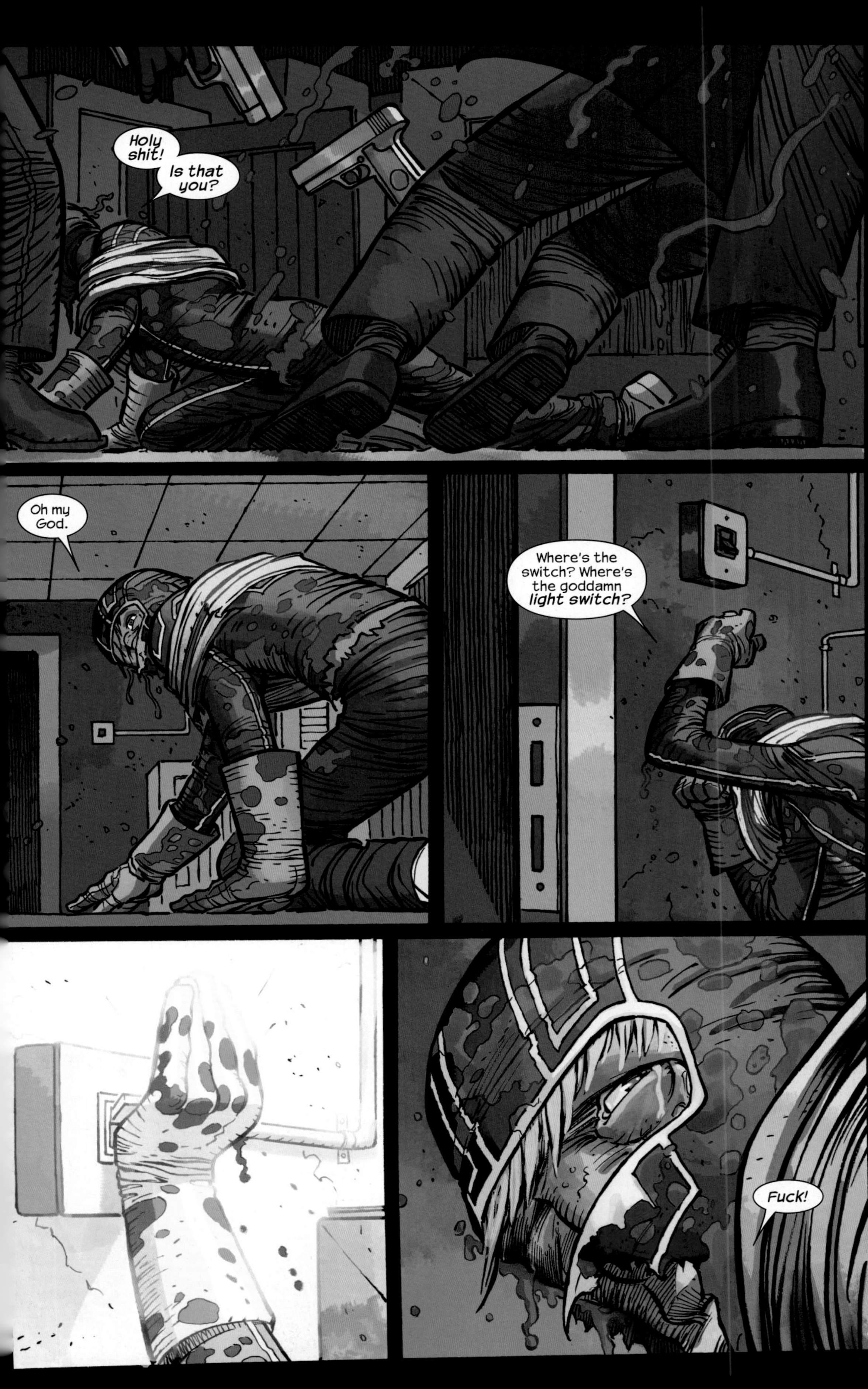
Holy shit!
Is that you?
Oh my God.
Where's the switch? Where's the goddamn light switch?
Fuck!

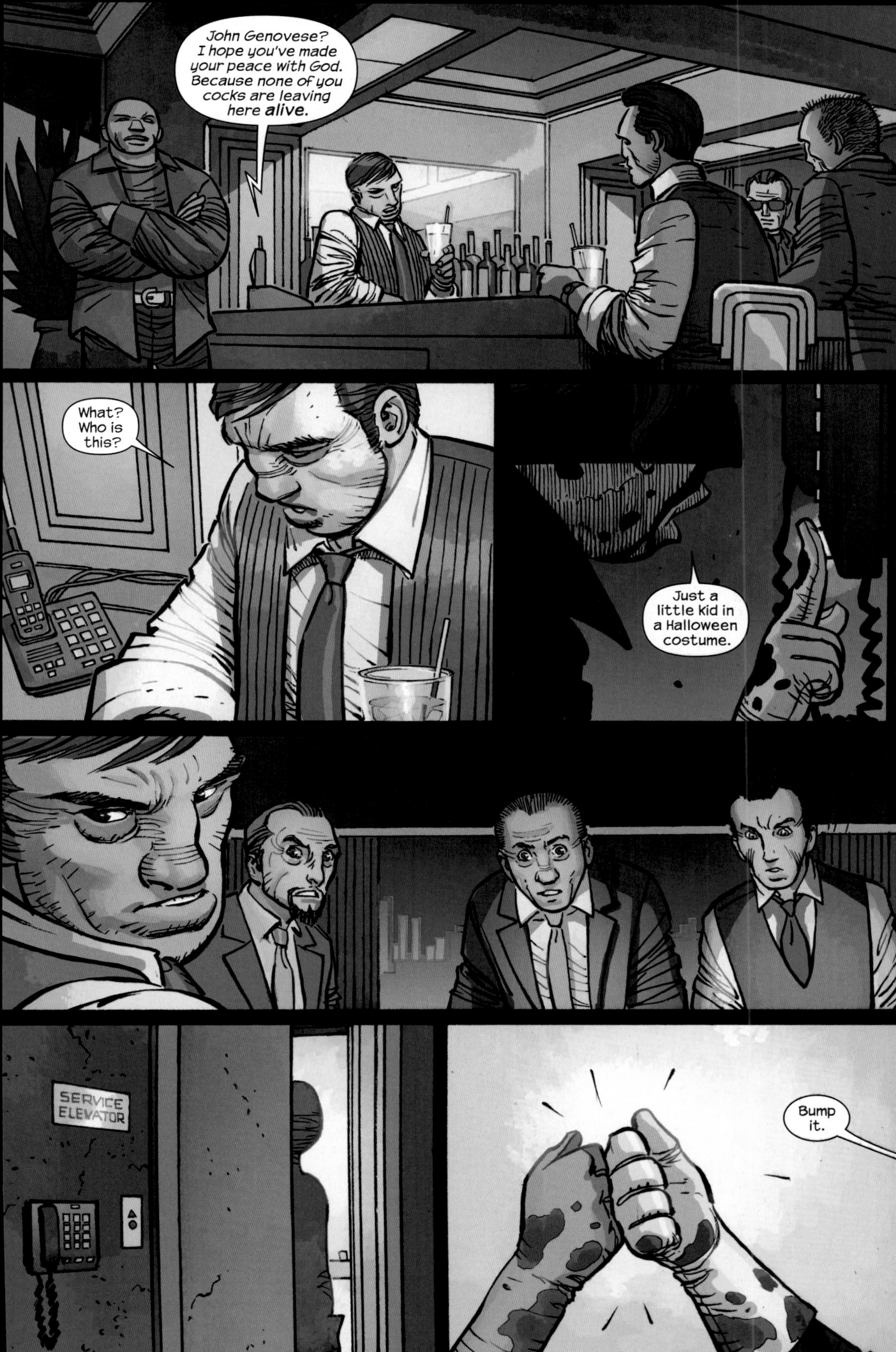
John Genovese? I hope you've made your peace with God. Because none of you cocks are leaving here **alive**.
What? Who is this?
Just a little kid in a Halloween costume.
SERVICE ELEVATOR
Bump it.

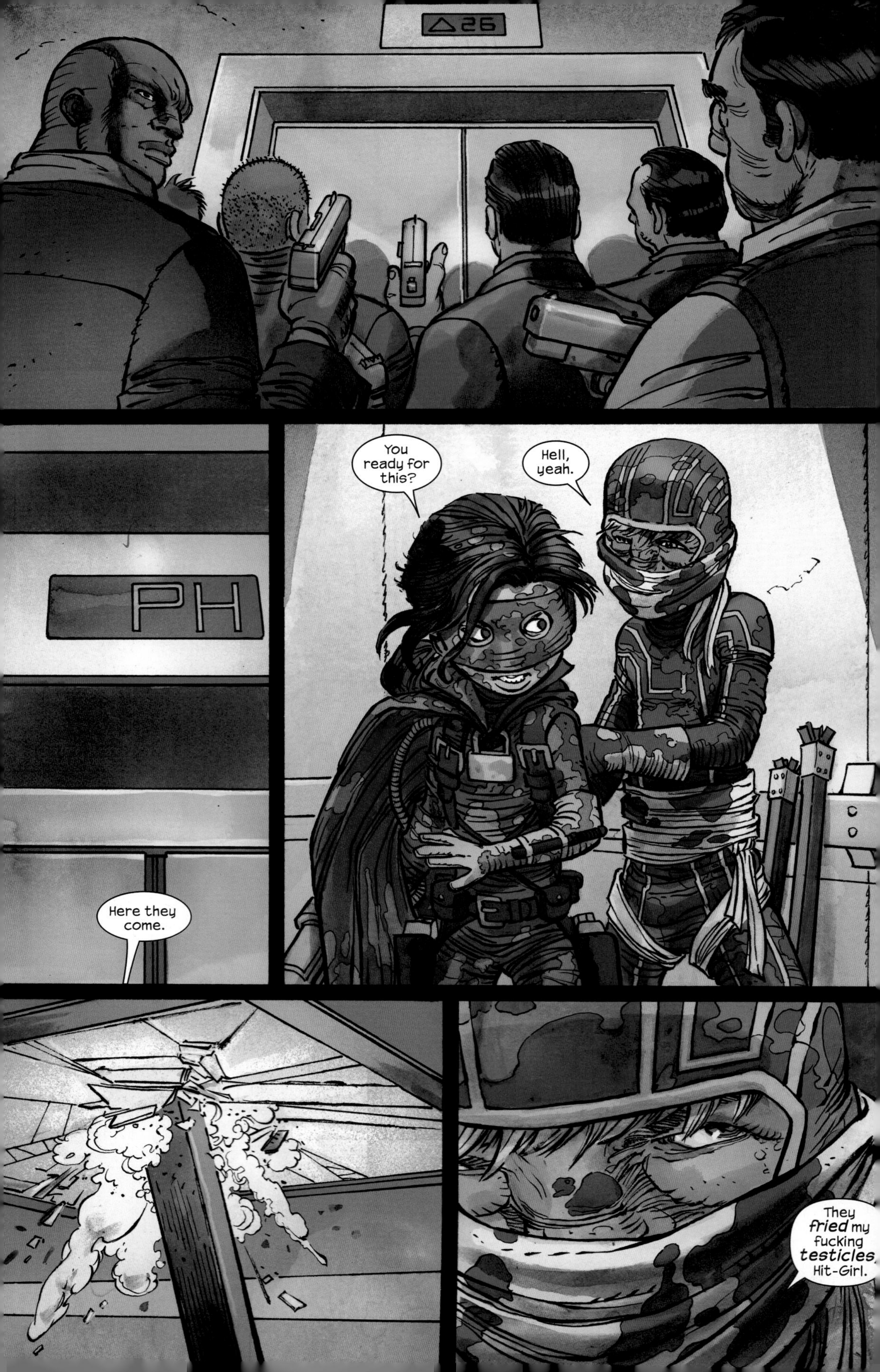

△26
PH
You ready for this?
Hell, yeah.
Here they come.
They *fried* my fucking *testicles*, Hit-Girl.

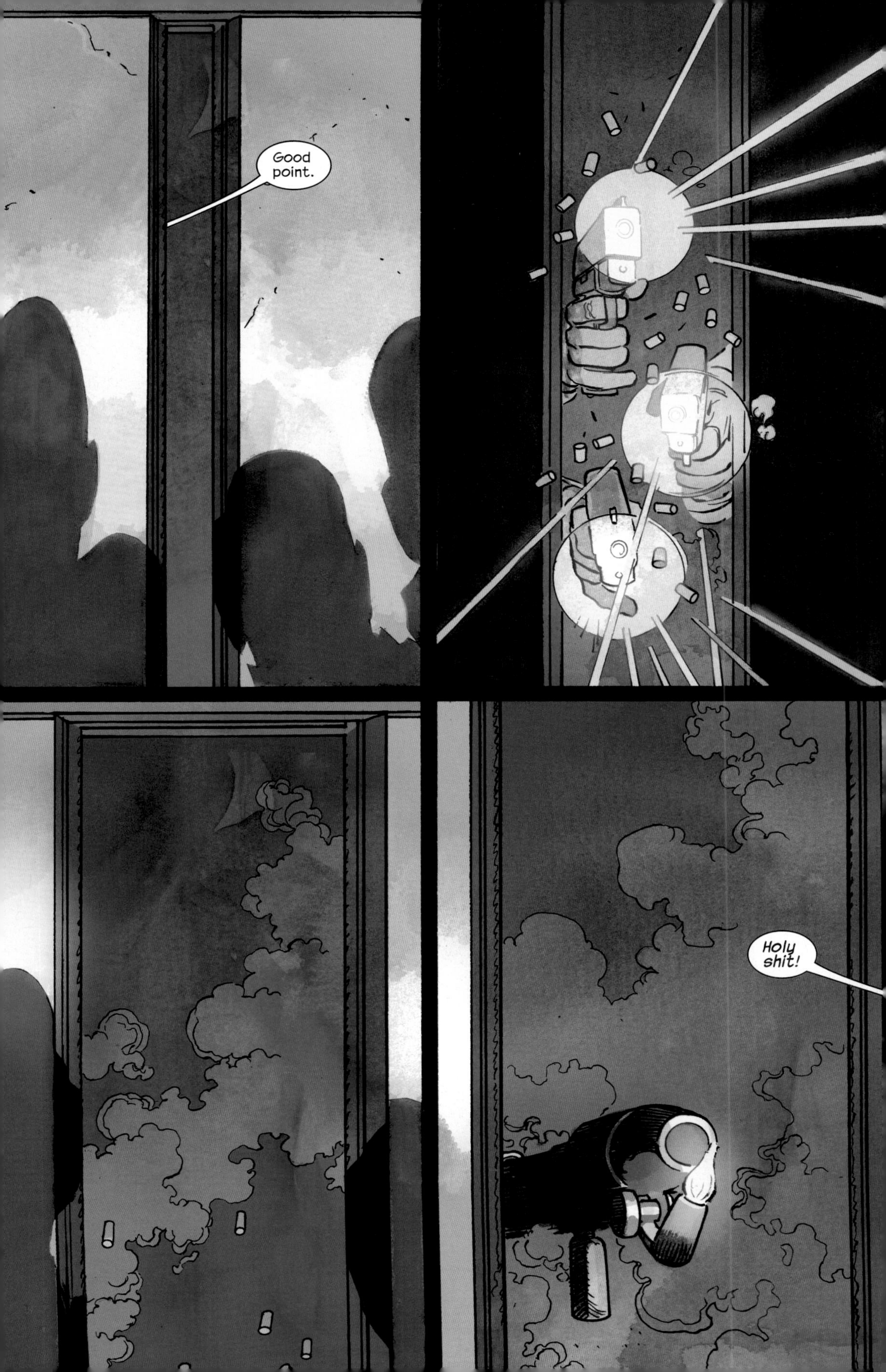
Good point.
Holy shit!

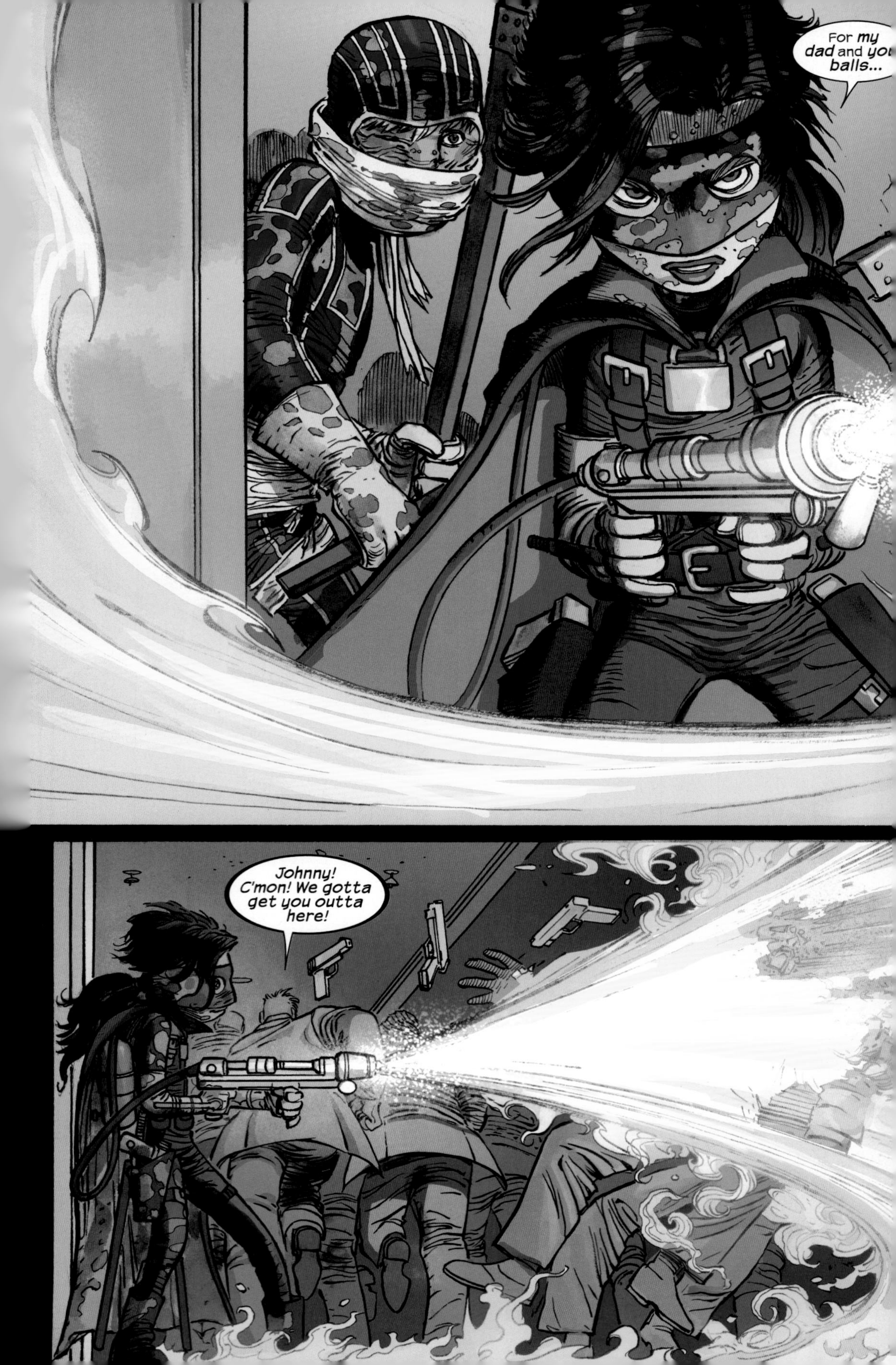
For my dad and yo
balls...
Johnny! C'mon! We gotta get you outta here!

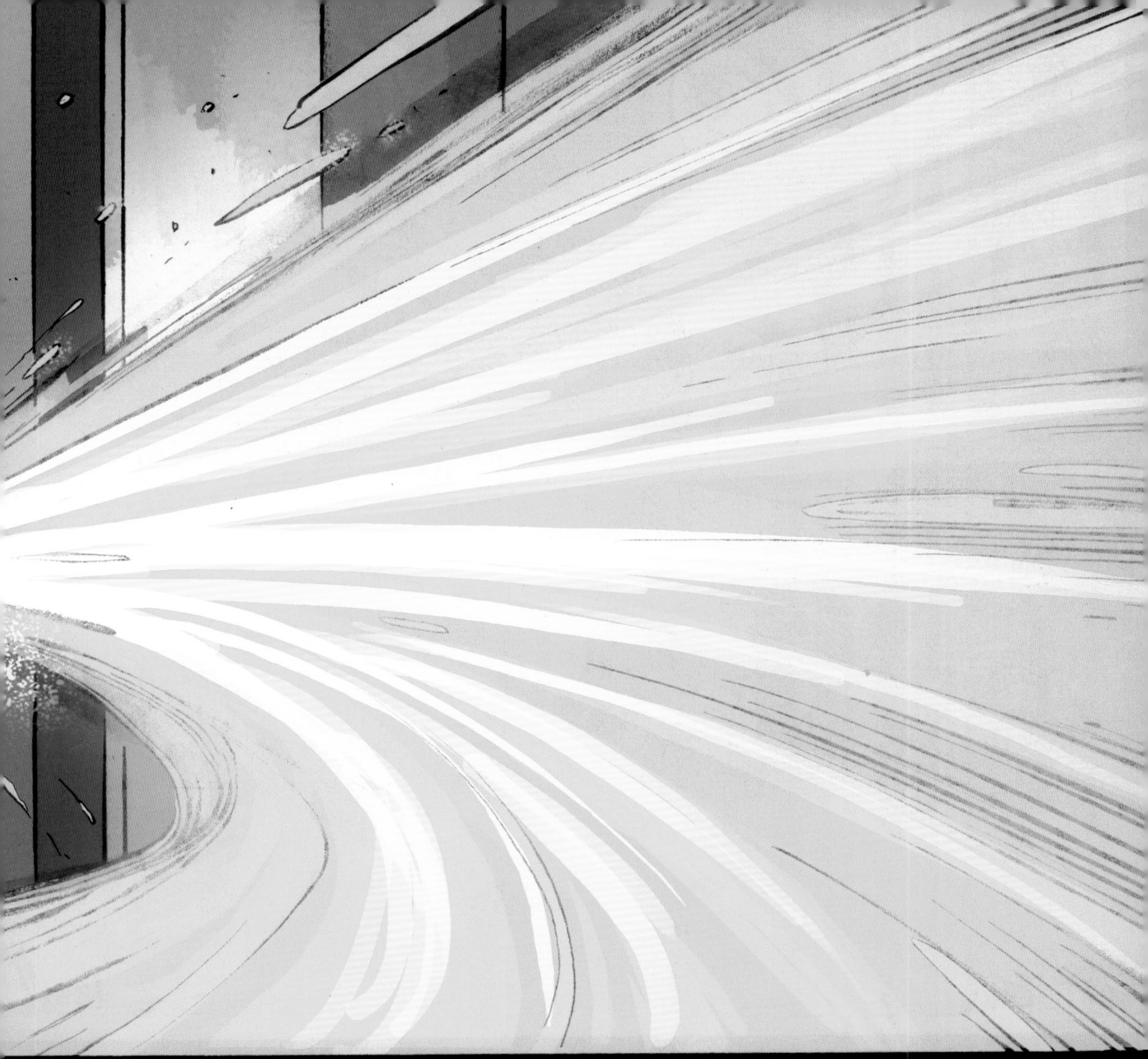

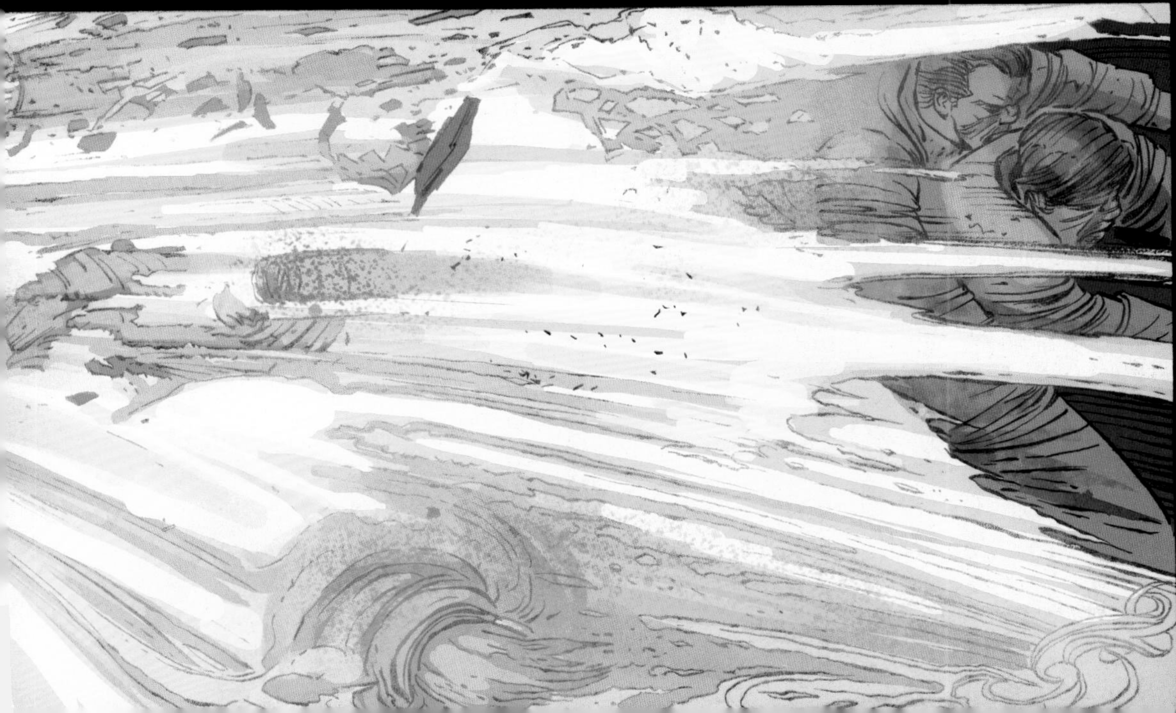

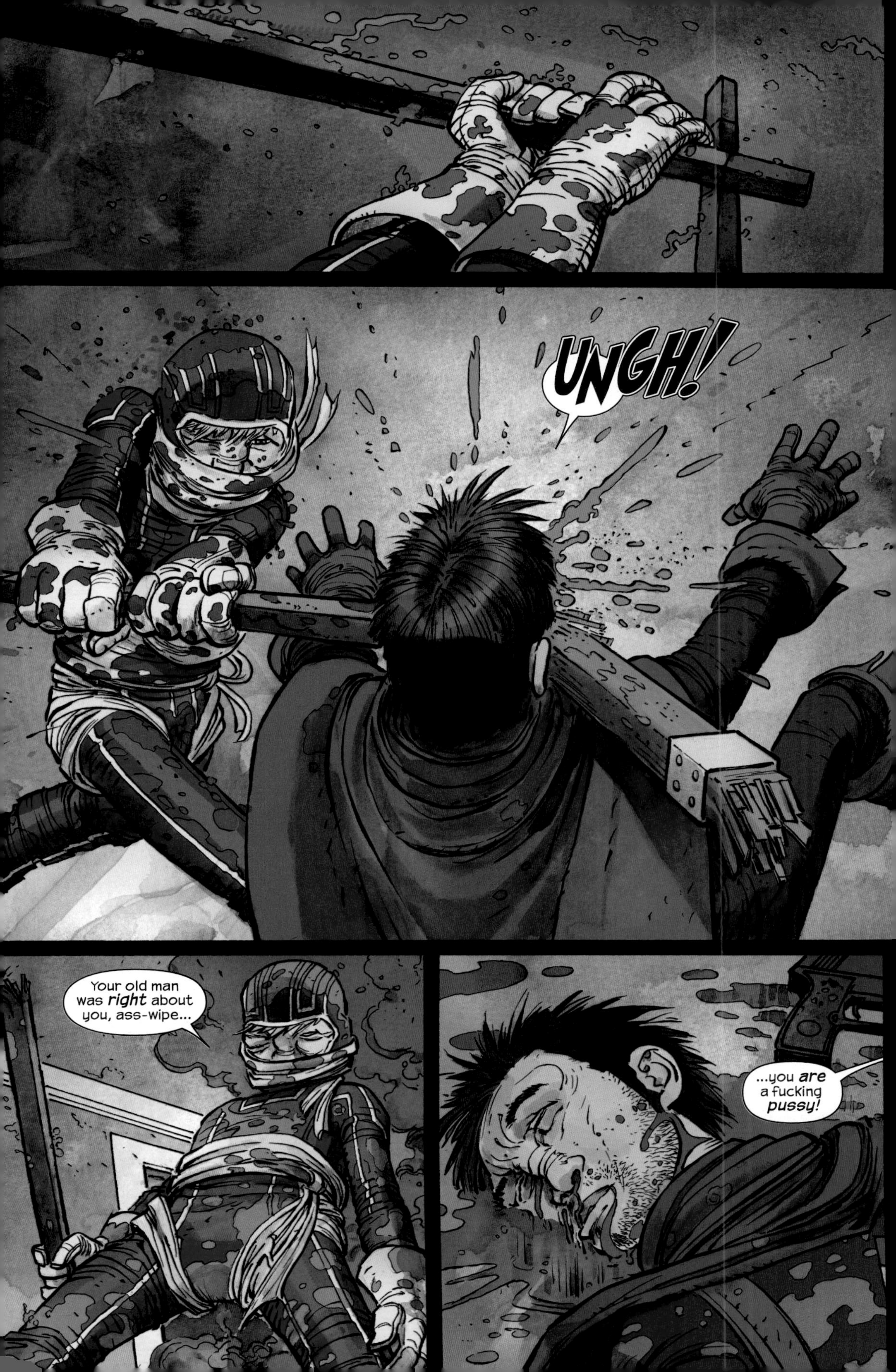
UNGH!
Your old man was right about you, ass-wipe...
...you are a fucking pussy!

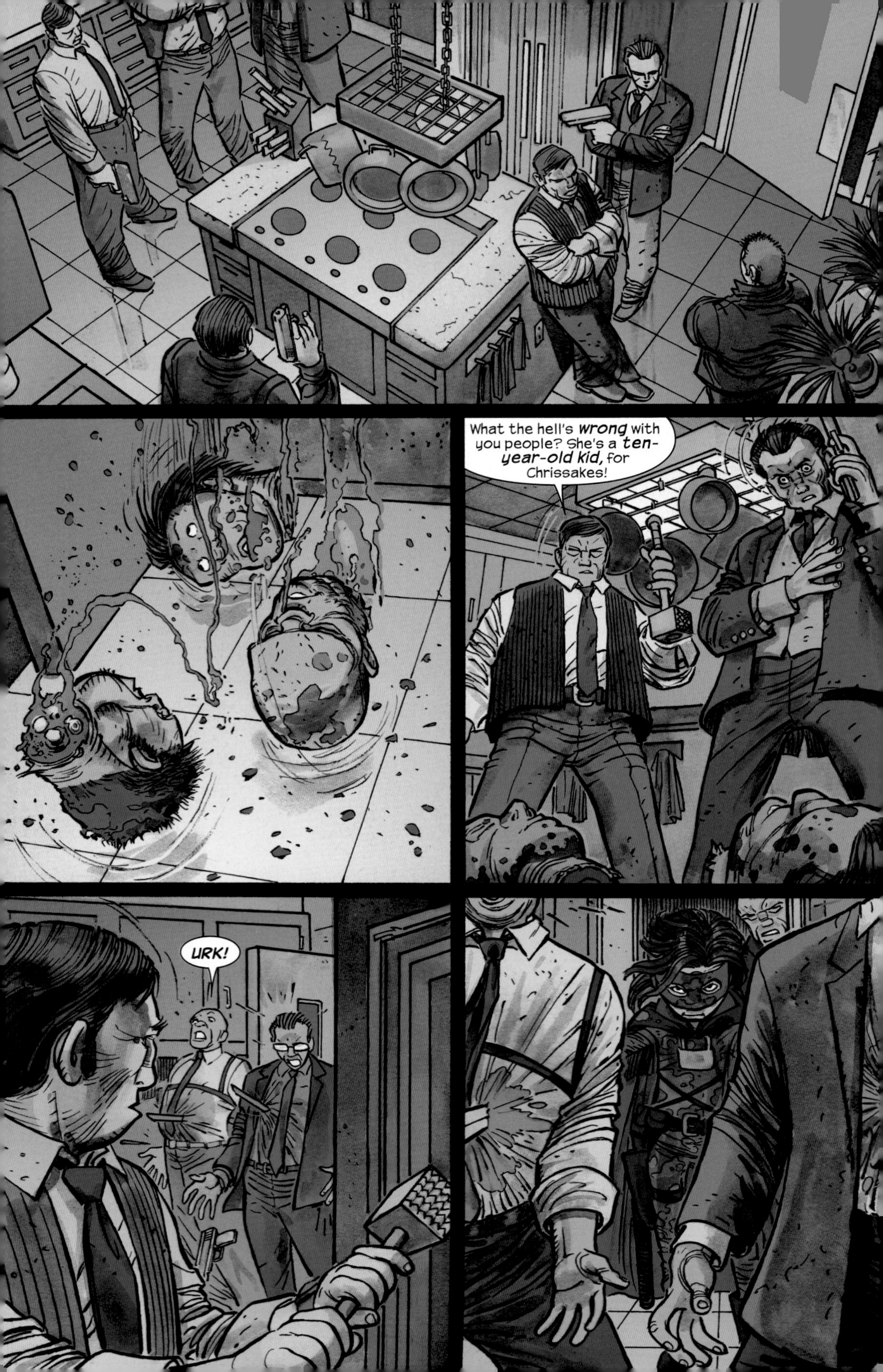
What the hell's wrong with you people? She's a ten-year-old kid, for Chrissakes!
URK!

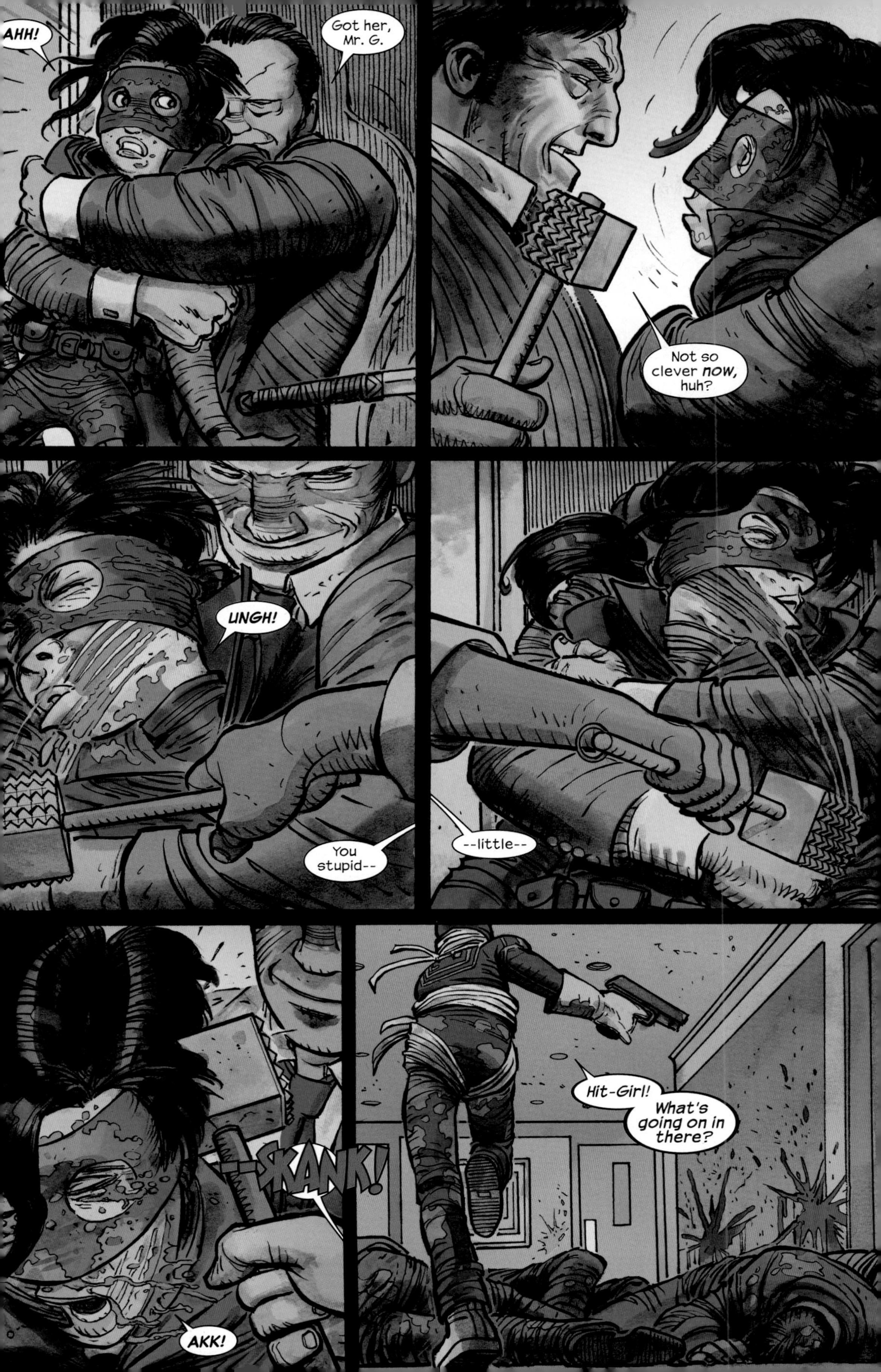
AHH!
Got her, Mr. G.
Not so clever *now,* huh?
UNGH!
You stupid--
--little--
SKANK!
AKK!
Hit-Girl! What's going on in there?

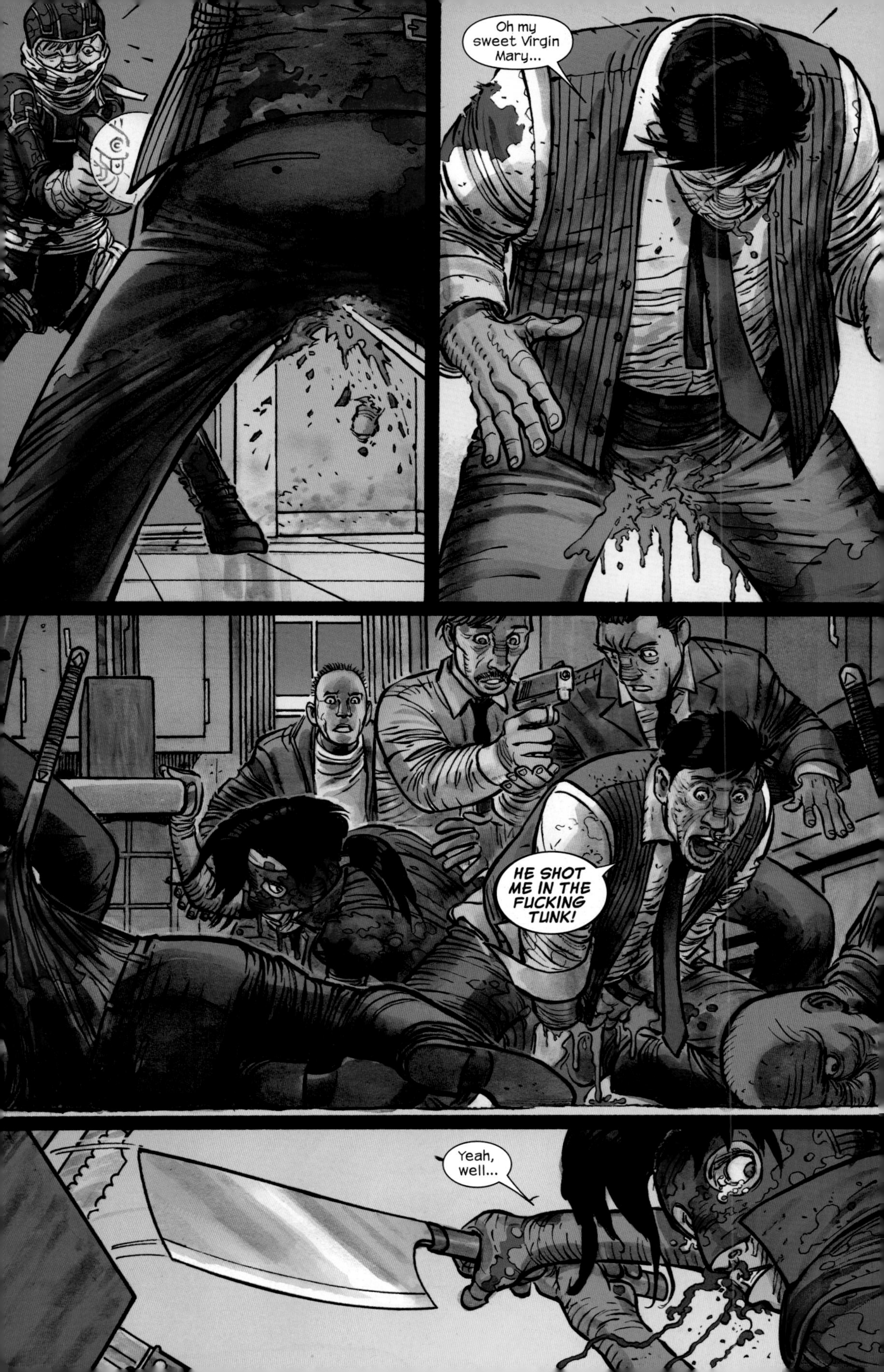
Oh my sweet Virgin Mary...
HE SHOT ME IN THE FUCKING TUNK!
Yeah, well...

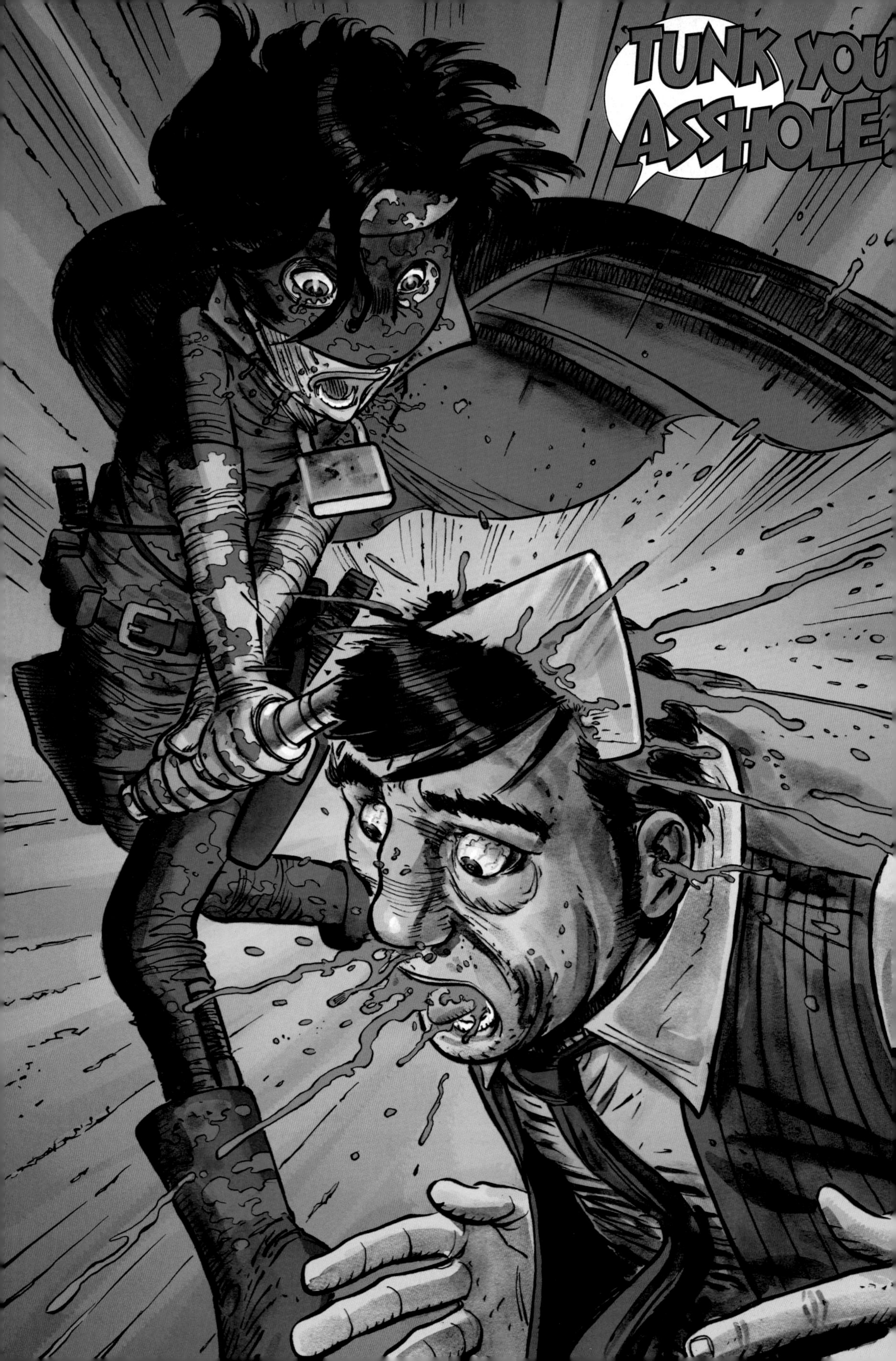
TUNK YOU ASSHOLE

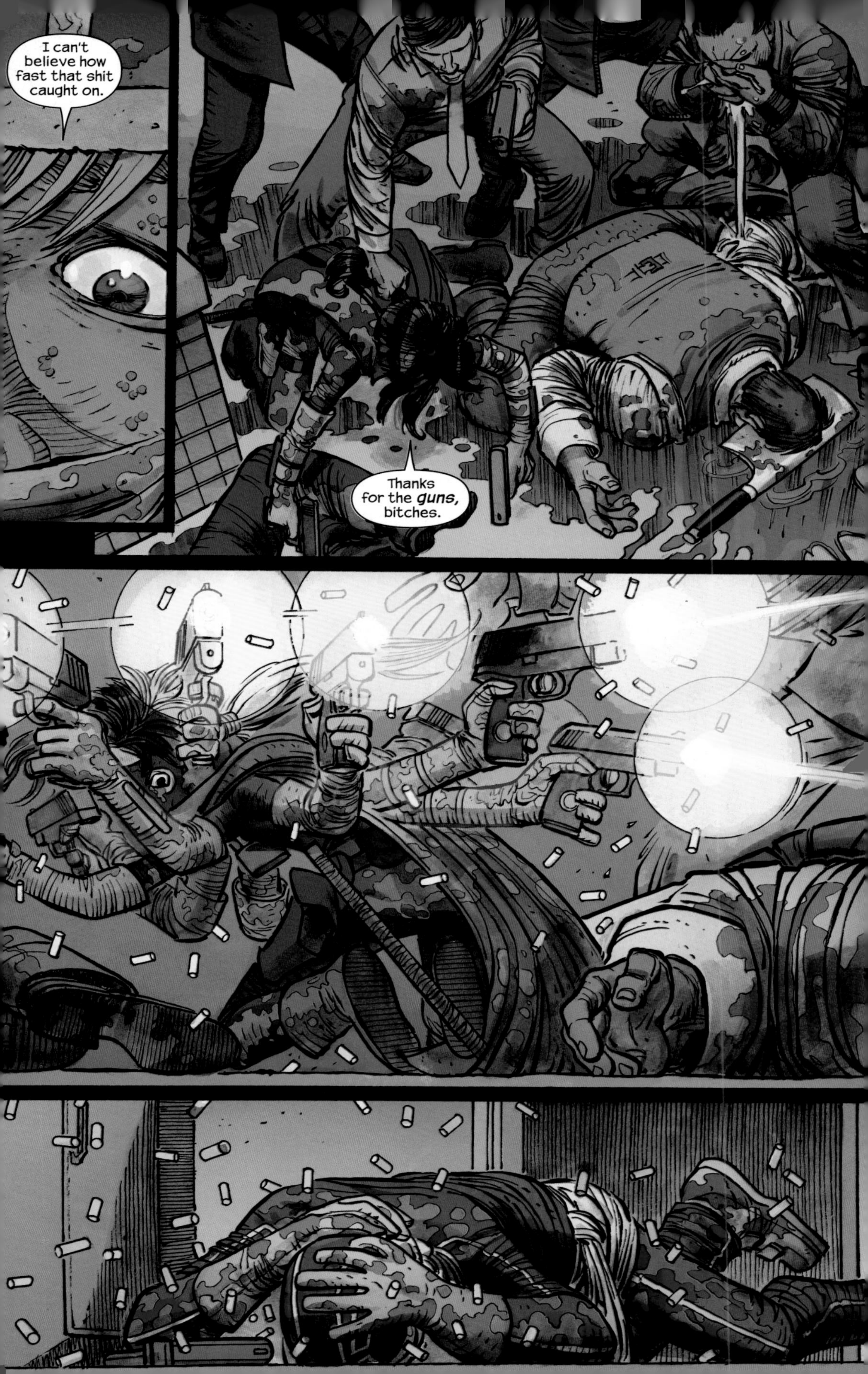
I can't believe how fast that shit caught on.
Thanks for the guns, bitches.

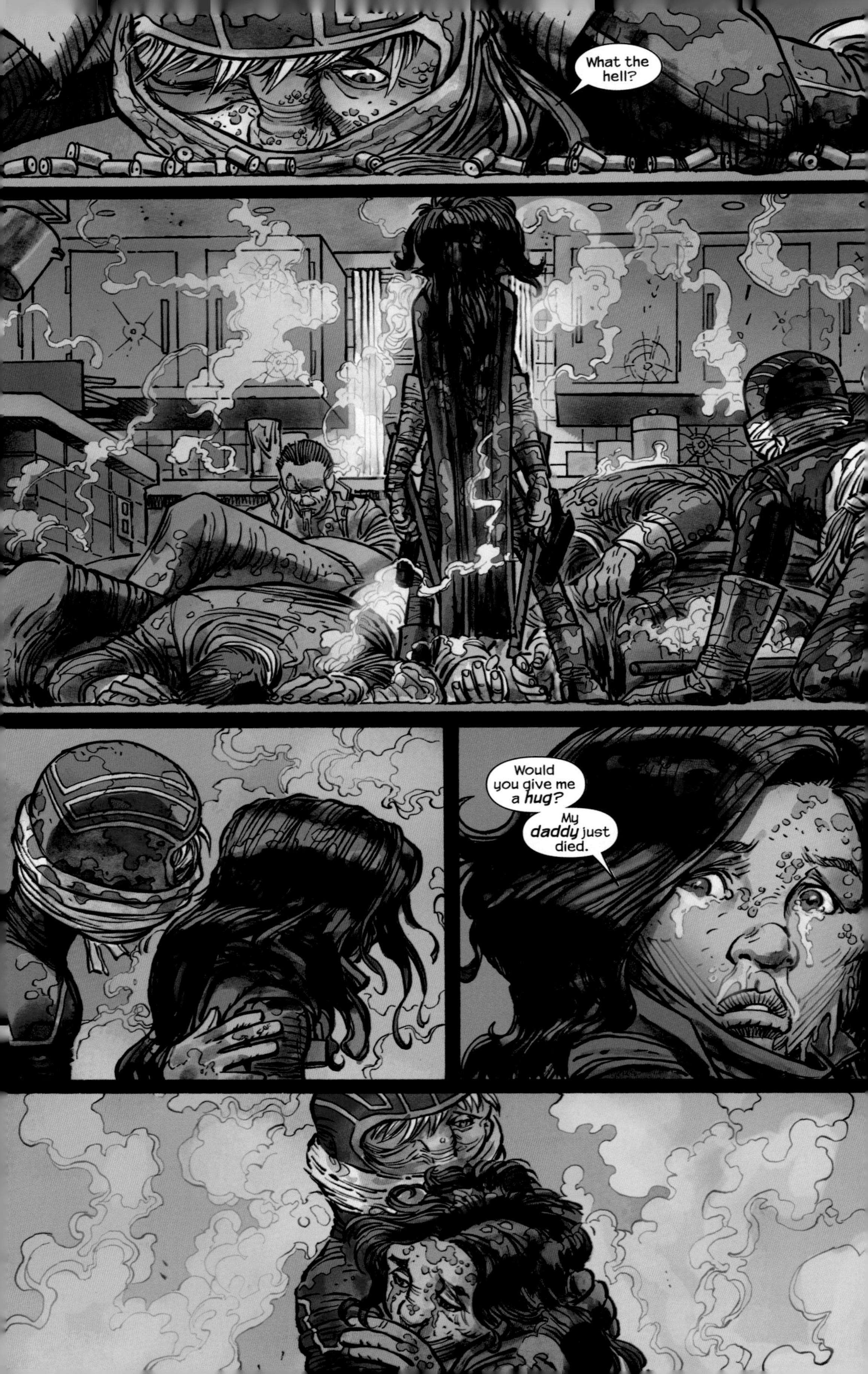
What the hell?
Would you give me a hug?
My daddy just died.

hirty-four stiffs were
und in that building and,
t like every other time
it-Girl took a life, the
hole thing was blamed
on *gang-related
violence.*

The cops knew
something was
going on, but word
online was they
actually kinda
liked it.

Hit-Girl and me became a
legend on those forums.

We were Batman and
Robin. Green Arrow
and Speedy. Wonder
Woman and that *dykey-
looking* chick she used
to hang out with in
the *forties.*

But Hit-Girl's
ambitions died
with her father.

She wanted to be
Mindy McCready
for a while and so
we tracked down the
mom who had never
stopped *searching*
and gave her back
the baby she was
missing.

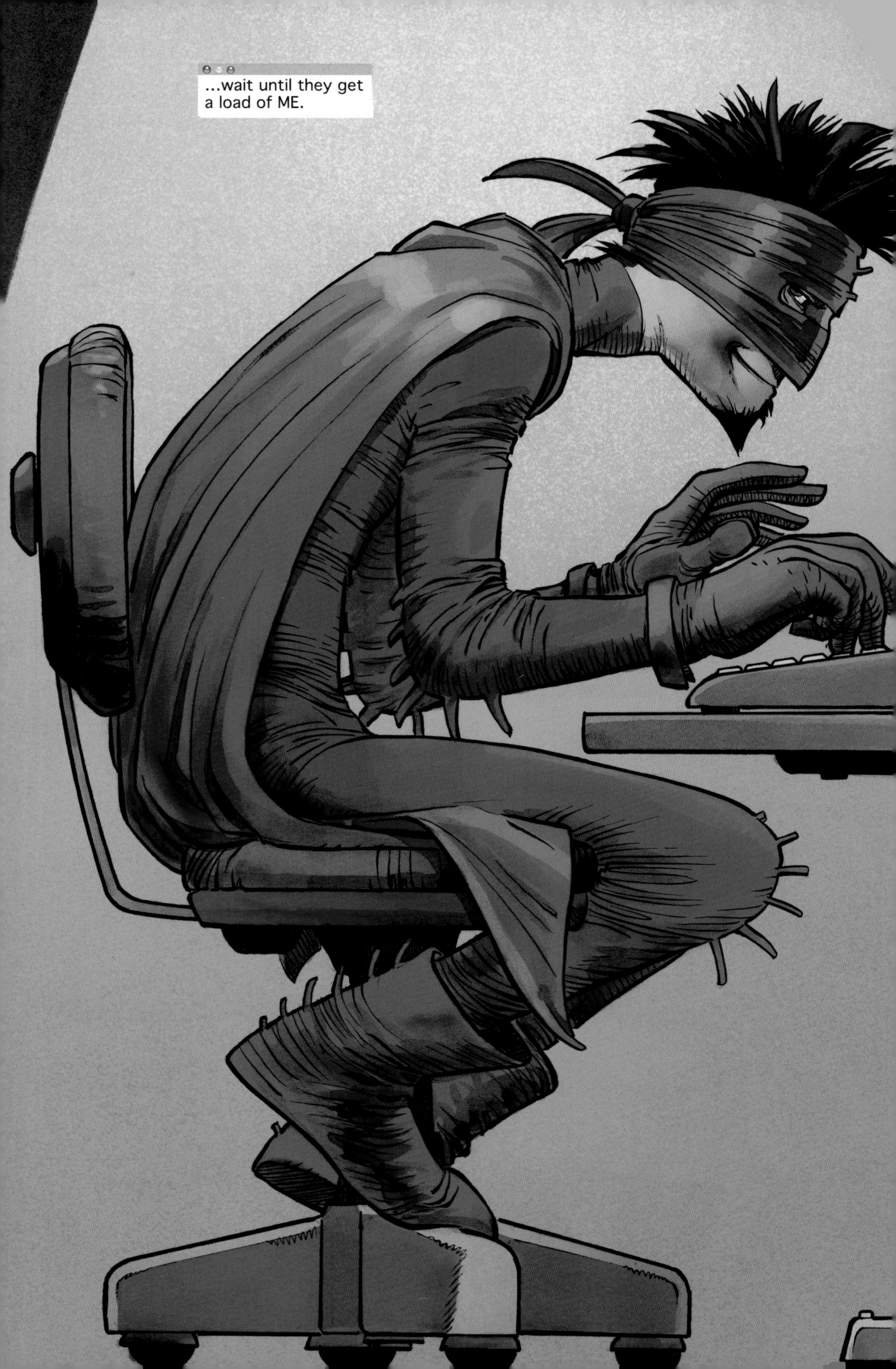
...wait until they get a load of ME.

END OF BOOK ONE

KICK

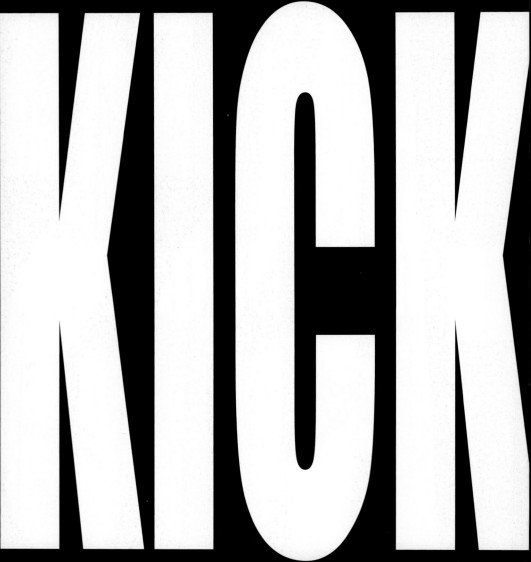

-ASS

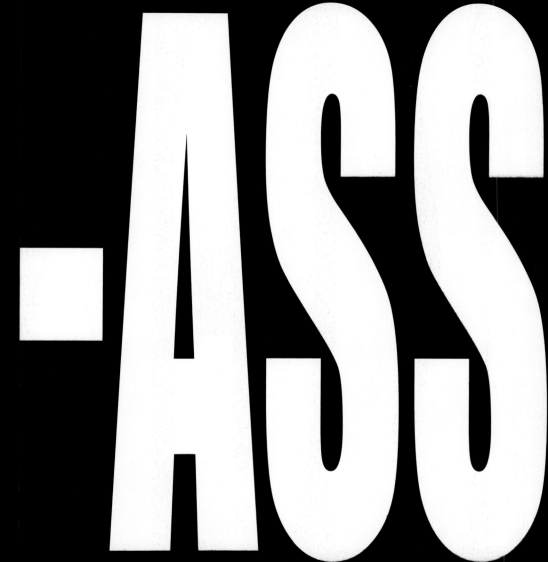

MARK MILLAR has been one of the key writers for Marvel Comics in the 21st century. Millar's first major contribution to Marvel was *Ultimate X-Men*, which achieved great creative and commercial success throughout his two-year run. Working with artist Bryan Hitch on *The Ultimates*, Millar surpassed his own success with that commercial and critical darling. Next, joining up with some of the industry's top creative talent, the Scottish writer took on two of Marvel's most iconic characters: Spider-Man and Wolverine. While working on creator-owned books like *Wanted*, turned into a Hollywood blockbuster staring Angelina Jolie, he penned *Civil War*, the epic miniseries that definitively reshaped the landscape of Marvel's heroes. More recently, Millar has reunited with Hitch on *Fantastic Four* and with *Civil War* artist Steve McNiven in both the pages of *Wolverine* and the upcoming *Nemesis*, as well as returning to the Ultimate Universe with *Ultimate Avengers*.

JOHN ROMITA JR. is a modern-day comic-art legend. A loyal Marvel artist since the late '70s, he has followed in his father's footsteps and helped keep the Romita name on the list of top-shelf talent. Timeless runs on *Iron Man, Uncanny X-Men, Amazing Spider-Man*, and *Daredevil* helped establish him as his own man artistically, and his art on *Wolverine* is arguably the decade's most explosive comic art—trumped perhaps only by his own work on the massive summer blockbuster event *World War Hulk*. JRJR has also paired with renowned writer Neil Gaiman for *The Eternals*, their reworking of the classic Marvel Comics characters, and has recently returned to *Amazing Spider-Man*; he will follow that up with another high-profile Marvel series.

TOM PALMER has worked as an illustrator in the advertising and editorial fields, but he has spent the majority of his career in comic books. His first assignment, fresh out of art school, was on *Doctor Strange*, and he has gone on to lend his inking talents to many of Marvel's top titles, including *X-Men, The Avengers, Tomb of Dracula*, and more recently *Punisher, Hulk,* and *Ghost Rider*. He lives and works in New Jersey.

AN WHITE is
e of the comic
ustry's best and
st sought-after
or artists. Well-
own for his work
titles such as *The
azing Spider-
n, Punisher, Dark
engers, Captain
erica, Black
nther, Wolverine
d countless more,
an's envelope-
shing rendering
d color palette
ng a sense of
ency and power
every page he
ches.

CHRIS ELIOPOULOS
is a multiple award-
winner for his
lettering, having
worked on dozens
of books during
the twenty years
he's been in the
industry—including
Erik Larsen's *Savage
Dragon*, for which he
hand-lettered the first
100 issues. Along
with his success as
a letterer, he also
publishes his own
strip *Misery Loves
Sherman*, wrote and
illustrated the popular
*Franklin Richards:
Son of a Genius*
one-shots, and writes
Marvel's *Lockjaw
and the Pet Avengers*
series.

MICHAEL HORWITZ's
student thesis (a five
minute documentary
about the private lives
of cabbages) was
met with resounding
indifference by
NYU, forcing the
Virginia native to
realize a career
in experimental
film wasn't in
the cards. With a
résumé padded to
the extreme (and
omitting a regrettable
excursion into the
world of go-go
dancing), Michael
somehow fooled
Marvel Comics into
hiring him, where
he now edits such
titles as Laurell K.
Hamilton's *Anita
Blake* and Stephen
King's *The Dark
Tower*.

JOHN BARBER
self-published his
own comics before
joining the world
of webcomics, and
later co-wrote a book
called *Webcomics*,
with Steven Withrow.
In 2003, Barber
joined the Marvel
Comics editorial team
and became editor
of the Wolverine
franchise, before
leaving to pursue a
freelance career—
including a return to
comics on the web
(webcomicsnation.
com/thejohnbarber).
He stuck around on
Kick-Ass, though,
which is a hell of
a way to go out,
editorially speaking.

BONUS CUTS

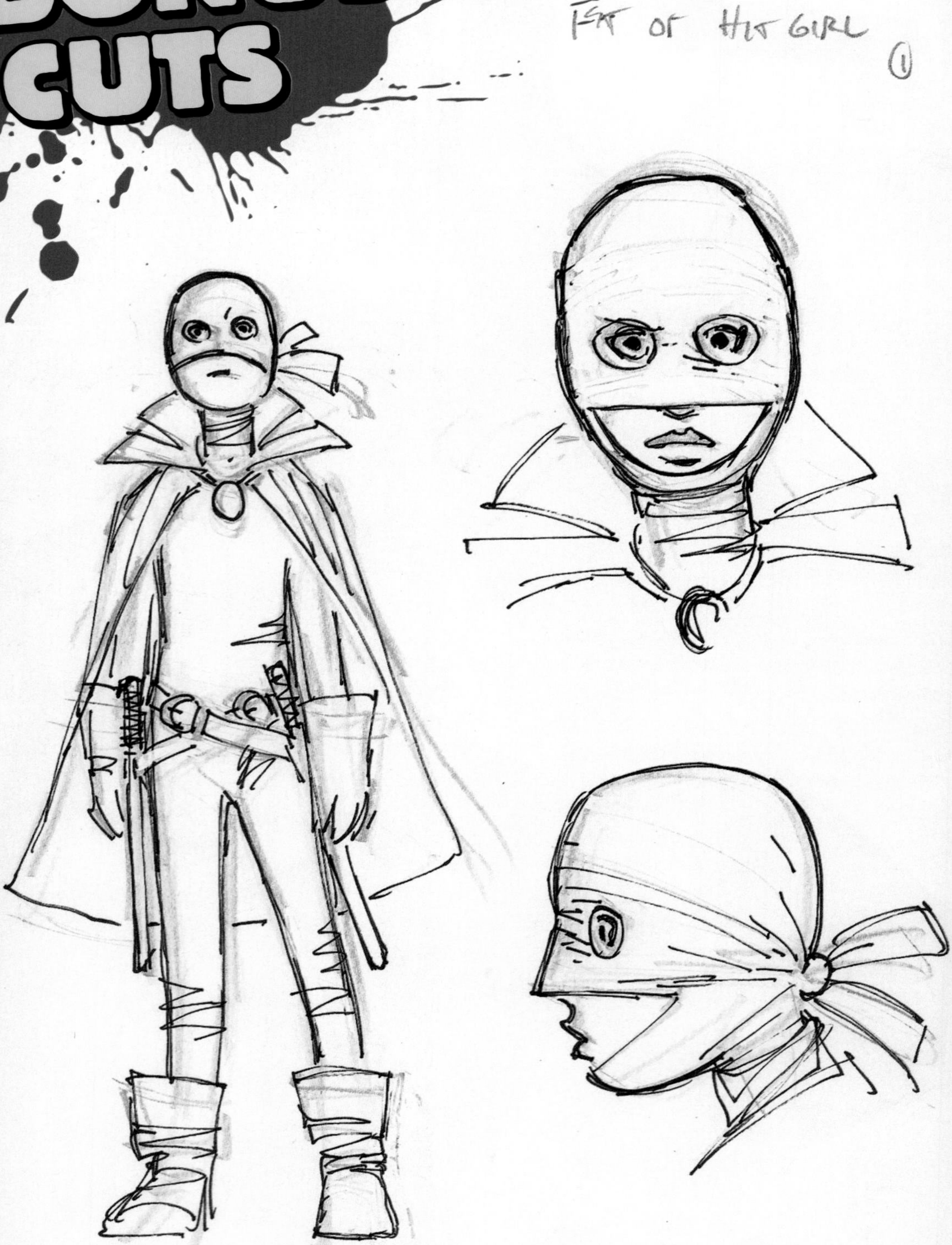
OF HIT GIRL
1

Early development sketches by John Romita Jr. of Hit Girl. All the elements are present even in this embryonic form: the cape, neckpiece and deadly blades. The main difference between this and the final design is the mask that covers her head.

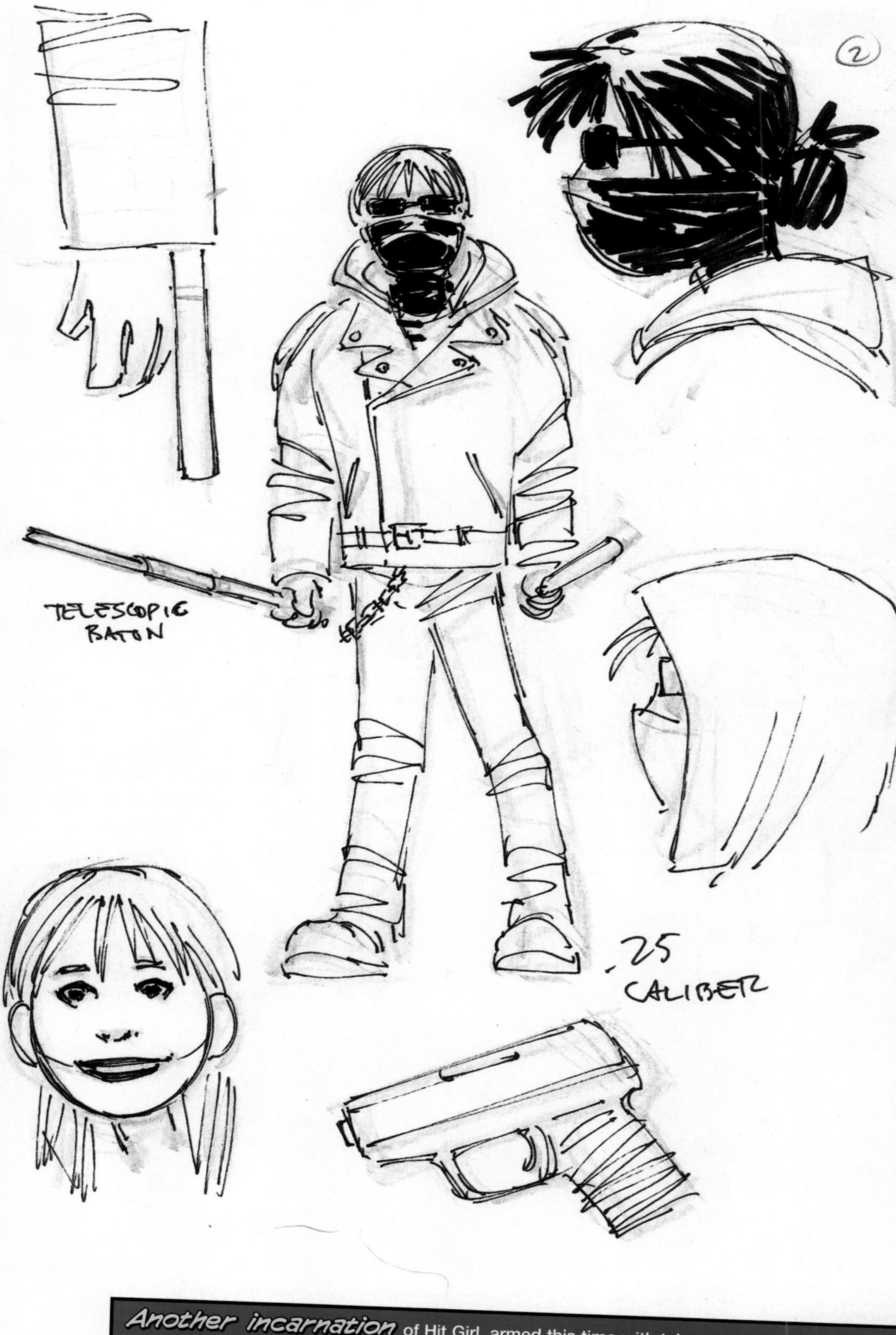

2
TELESCOPIC BATON
.25 CALIBER

Another incarnation of Hit Girl, armed this time with telescopic batons. The face mask now covers her mouth, and the cape has been replaced with a biker's leather jacket.

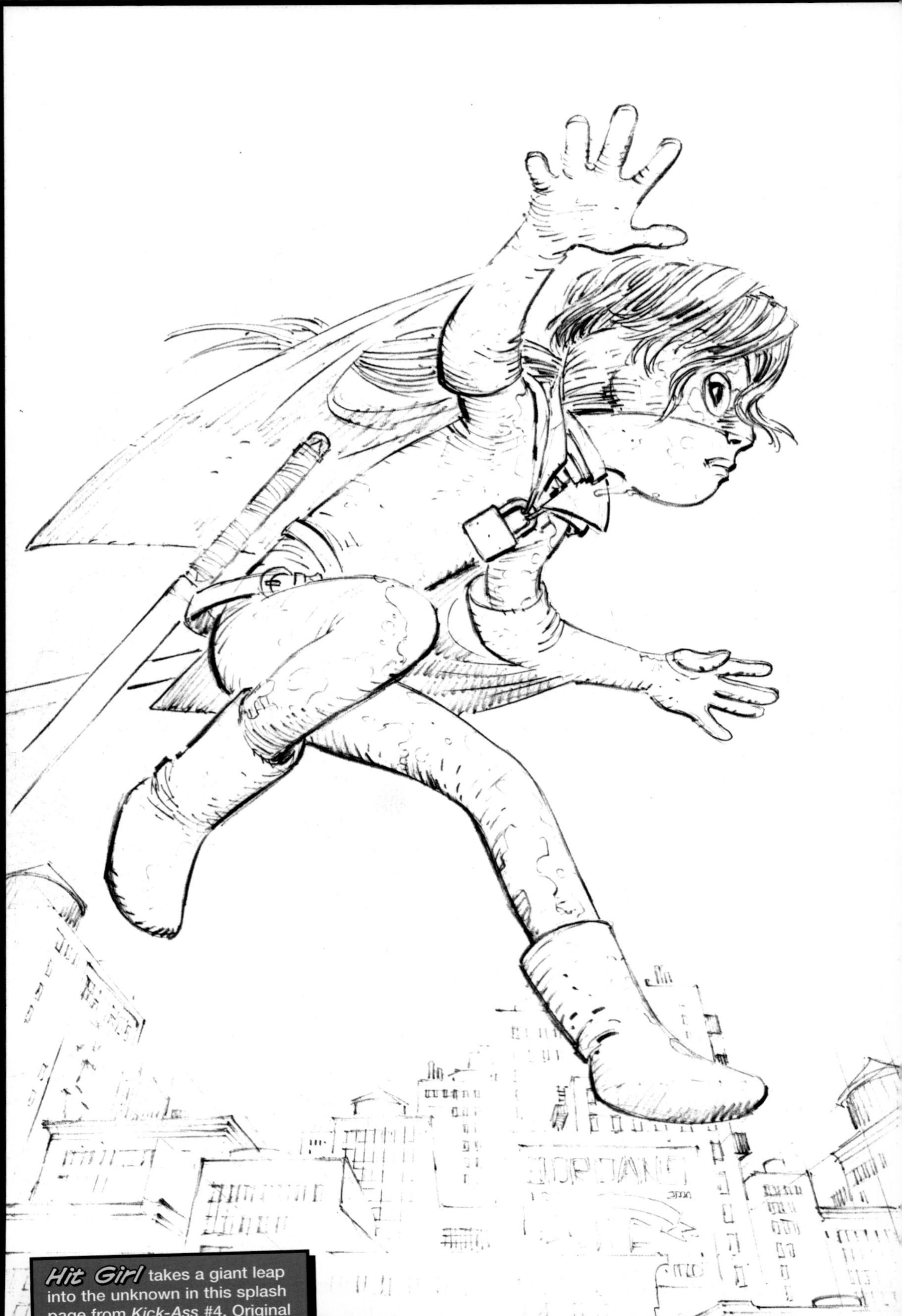

Hit Girl takes a giant leap into the unknown in this splash page from *Kick-Ass* #4. Original pencils by John Romita Jr.

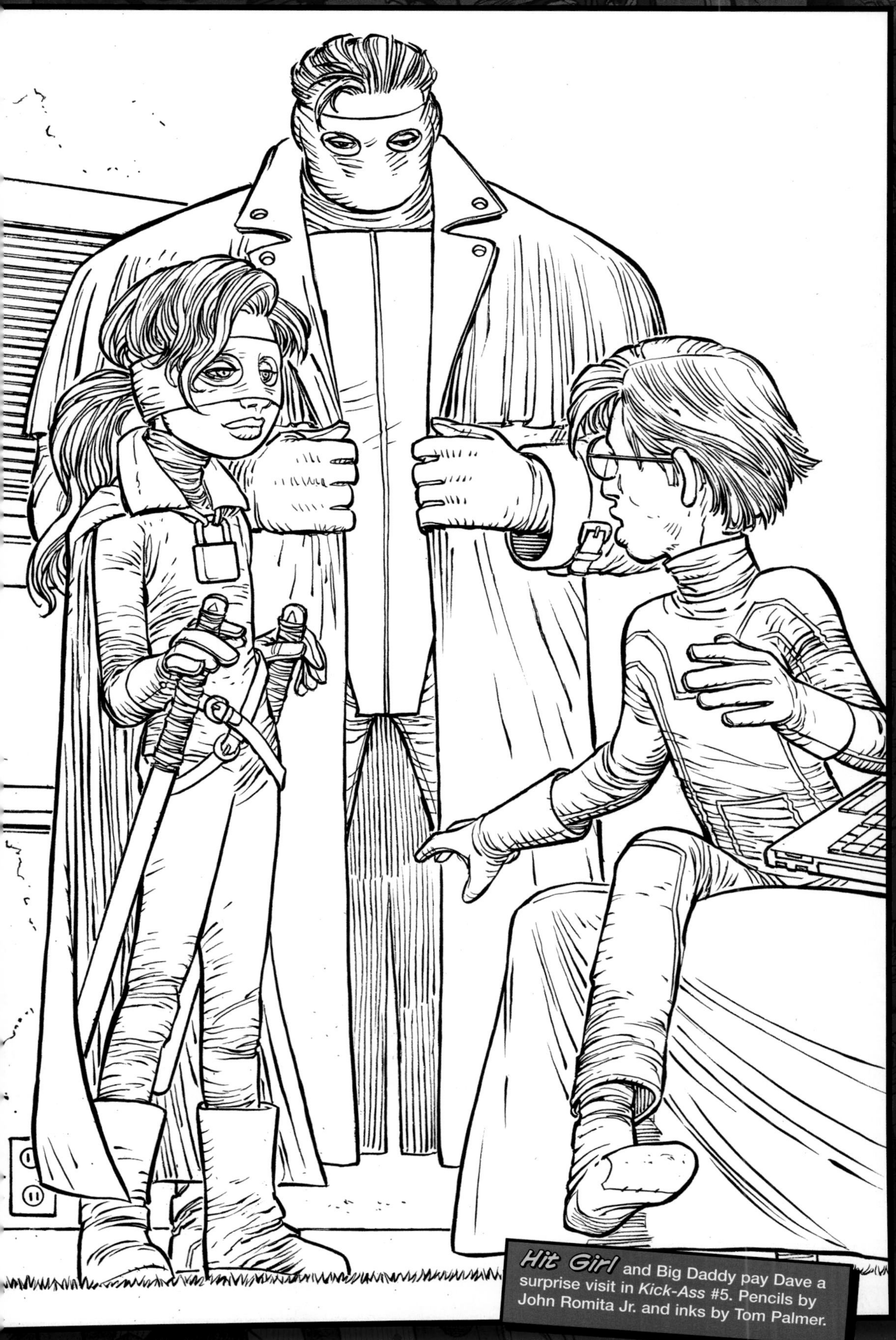

Hit Girl and Big Daddy pay Dave a surprise visit in *Kick-Ass* #5. Pencils by John Romita Jr. and inks by Tom Palmer.

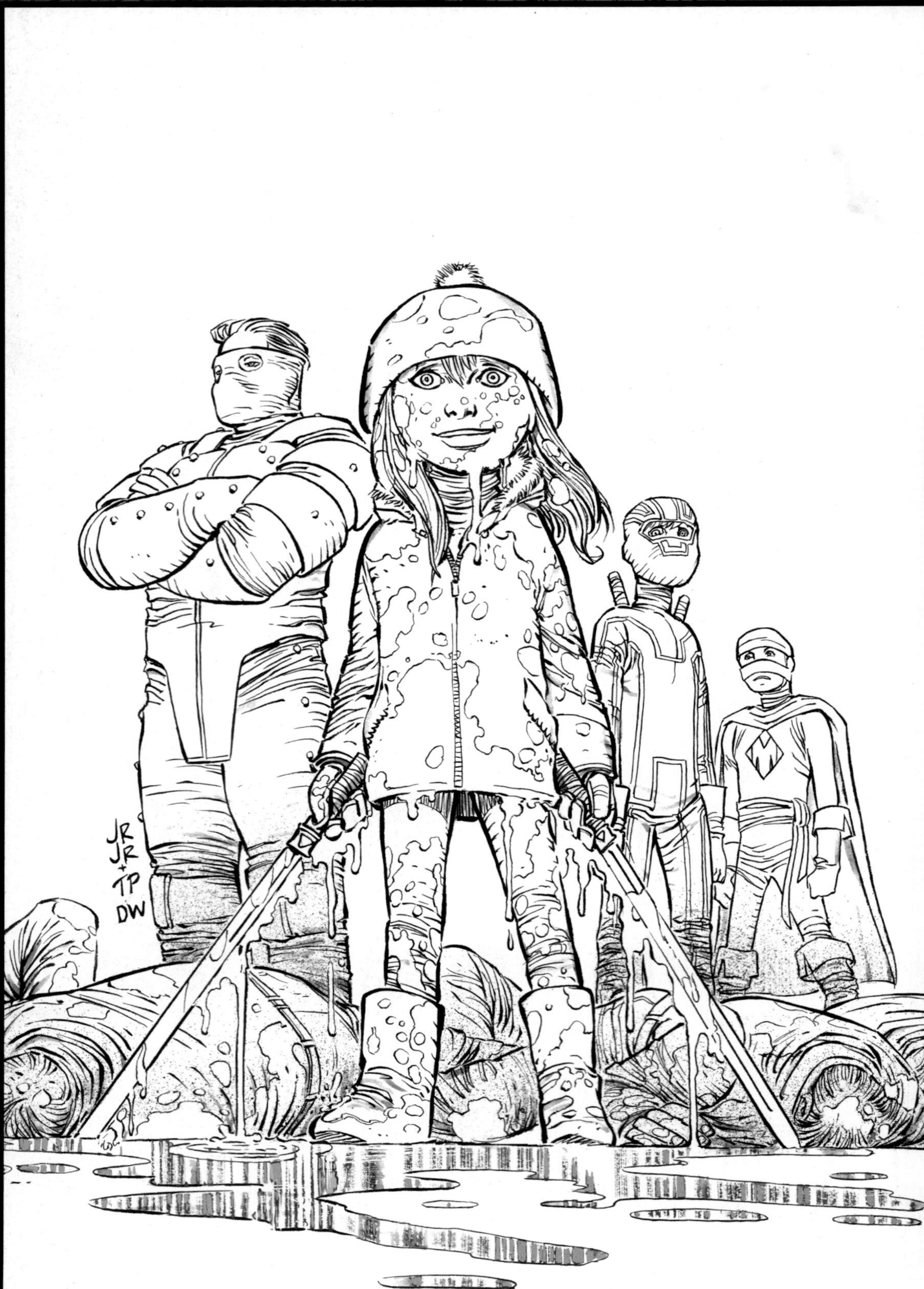
JR
JR
+
TP
DW

Hit Girl gets down and dirty on the original inked version of *Kick-Ass* #6's cover. Pencils by John Romita Jr. and inks by Tom Palmer.

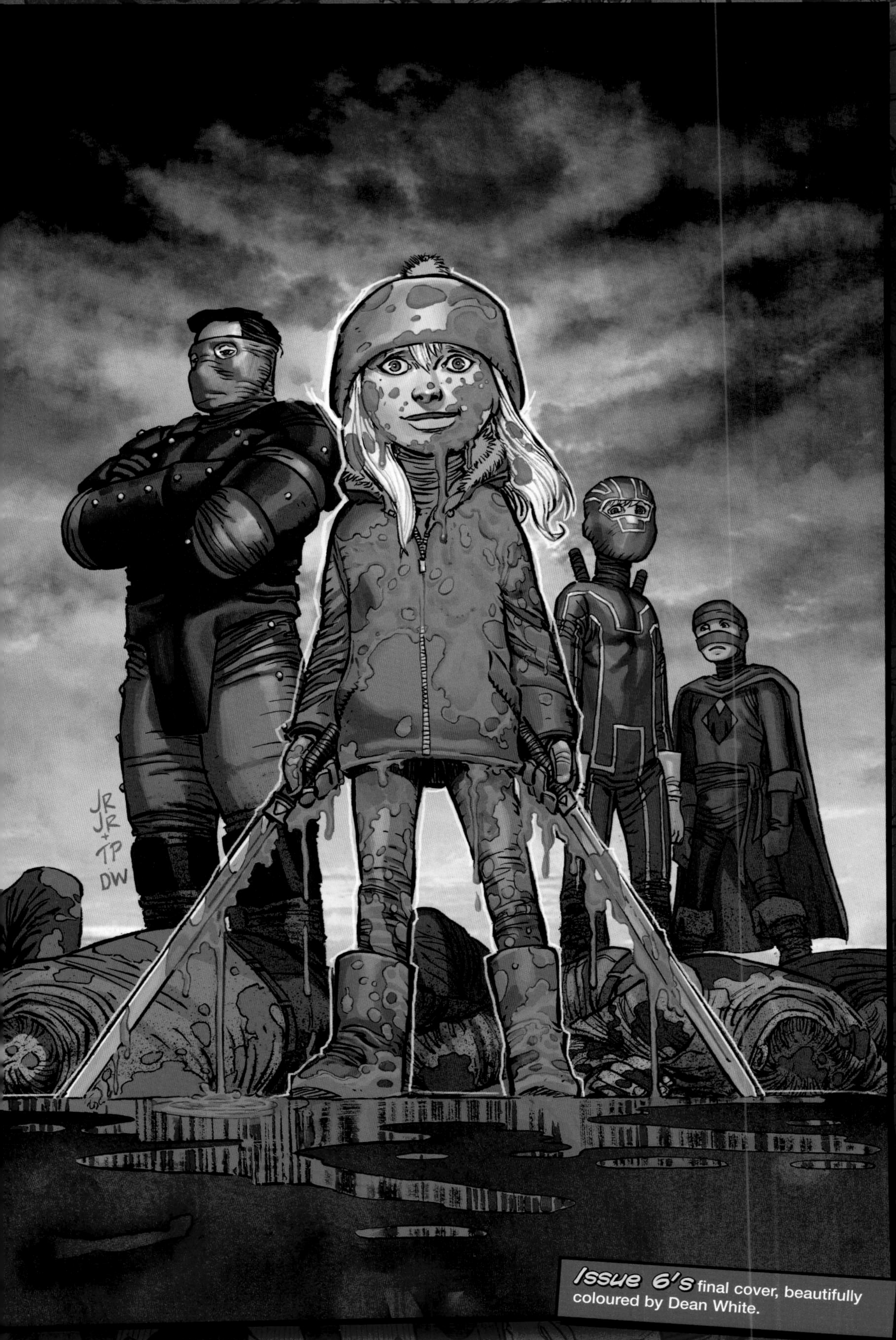
JR
JR
+
TP
DW

Issue 6's final cover, beautifully coloured by Dean White.

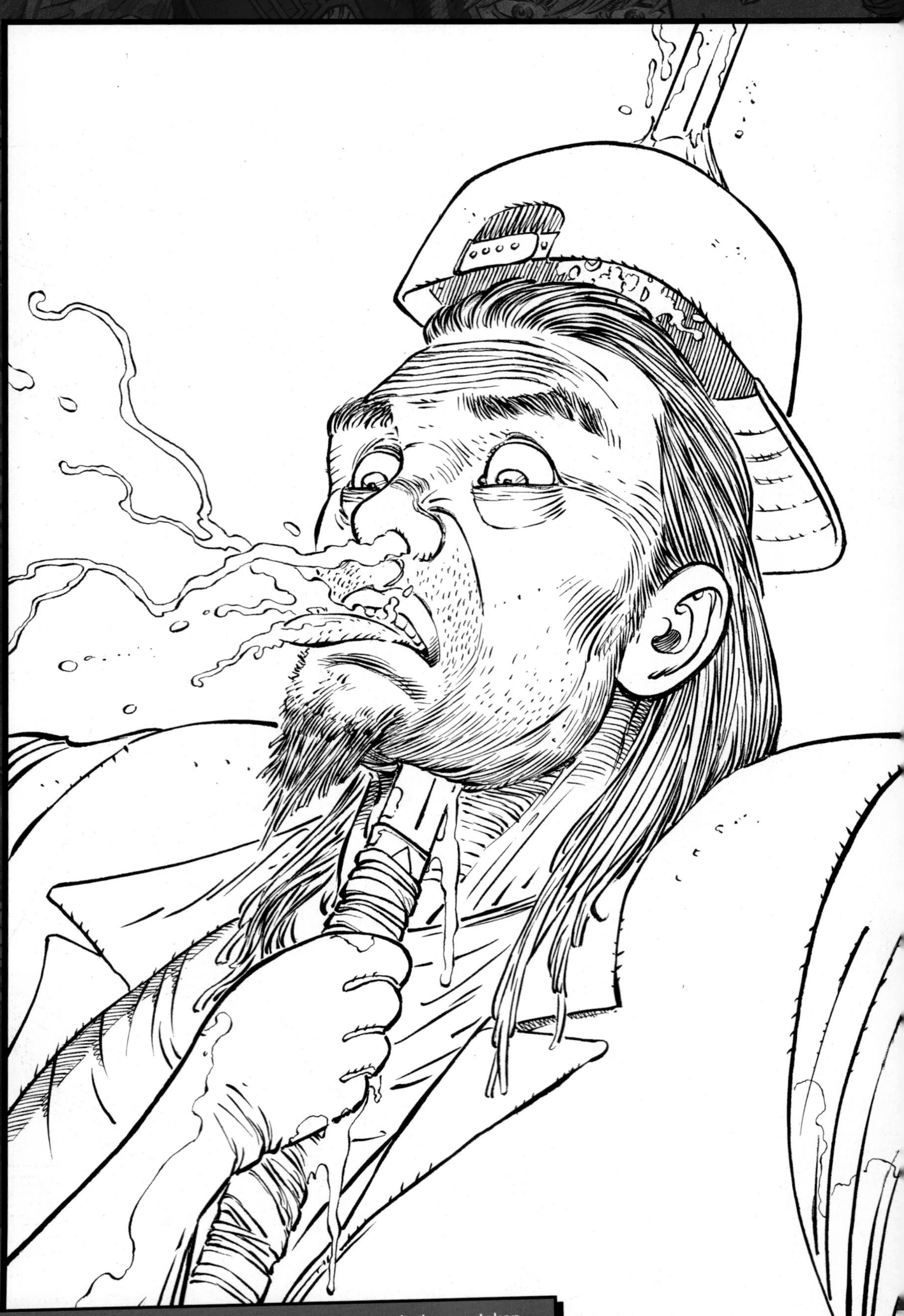

Hit Girl cuts to the chase in a shocking splash page taken from issue #4. Pencils by John Romita Jr. and inks by Tom Palmer.

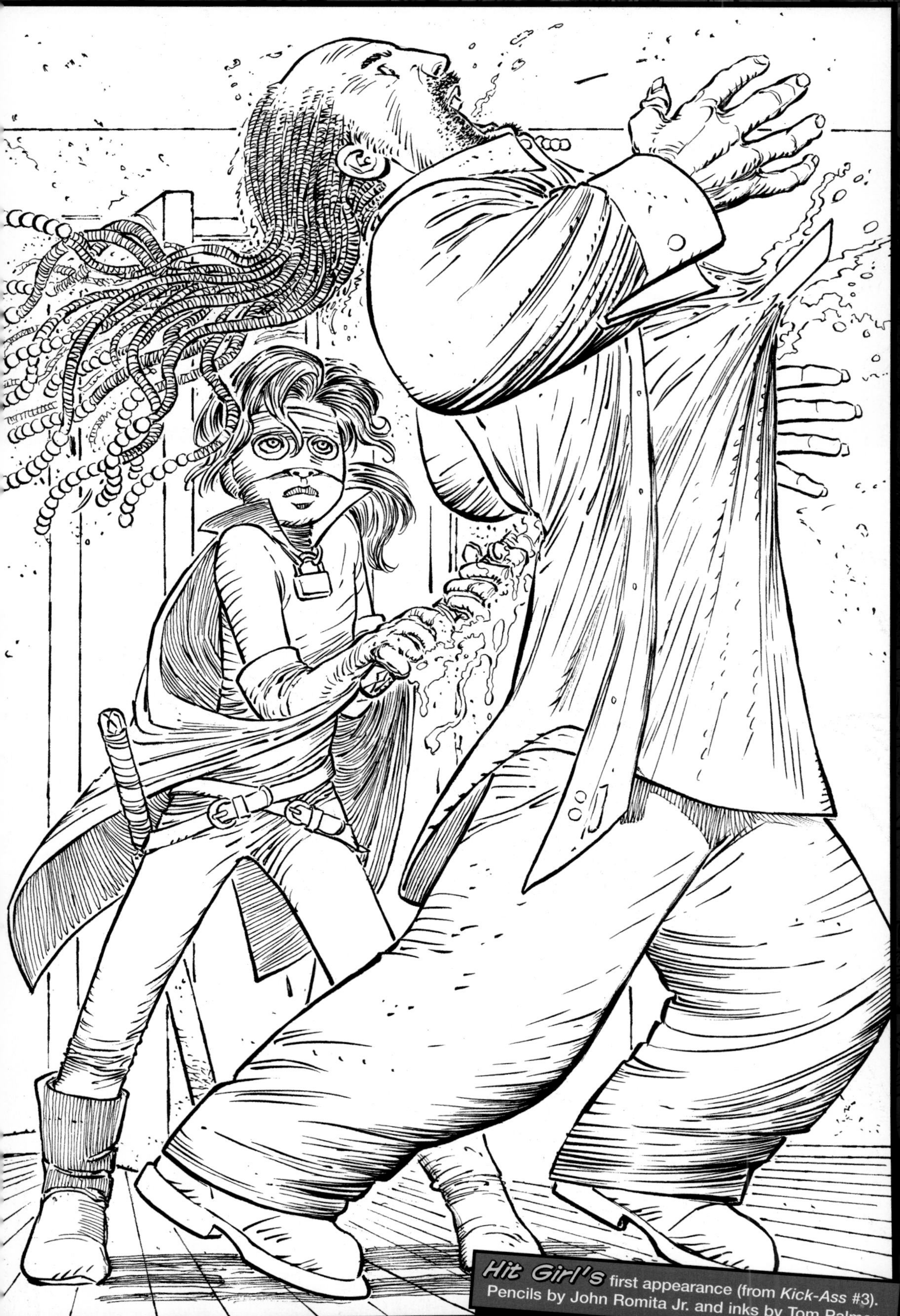

Hit Girl's first appearance (from *Kick-Ass* #3). Pencils by John Romita Jr. and inks by Tom Palmer.

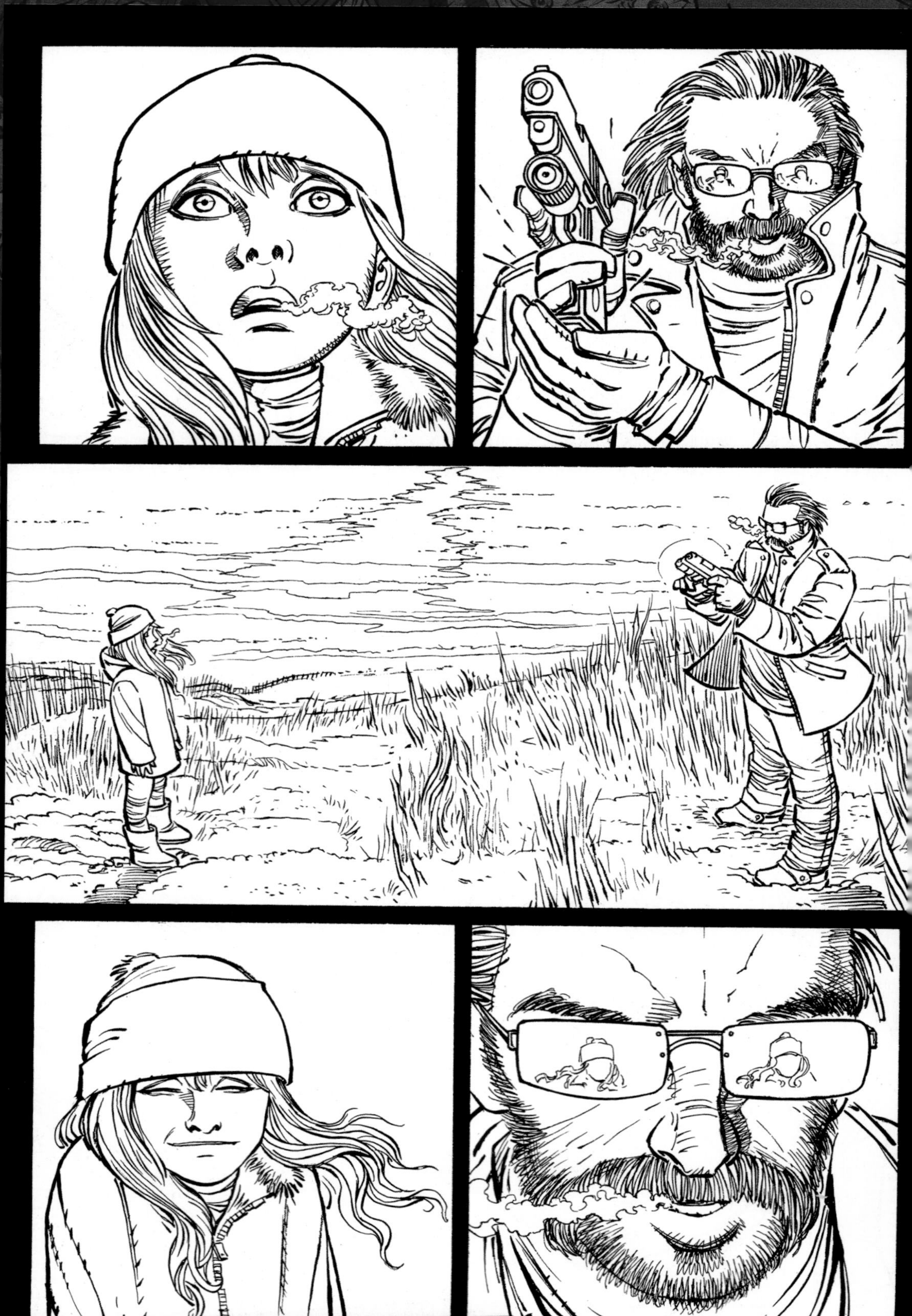

A sequence from Hit Girl's origin, taken from issue #6.
Pencils by John Romita Jr. and inks by Tom Palmer.

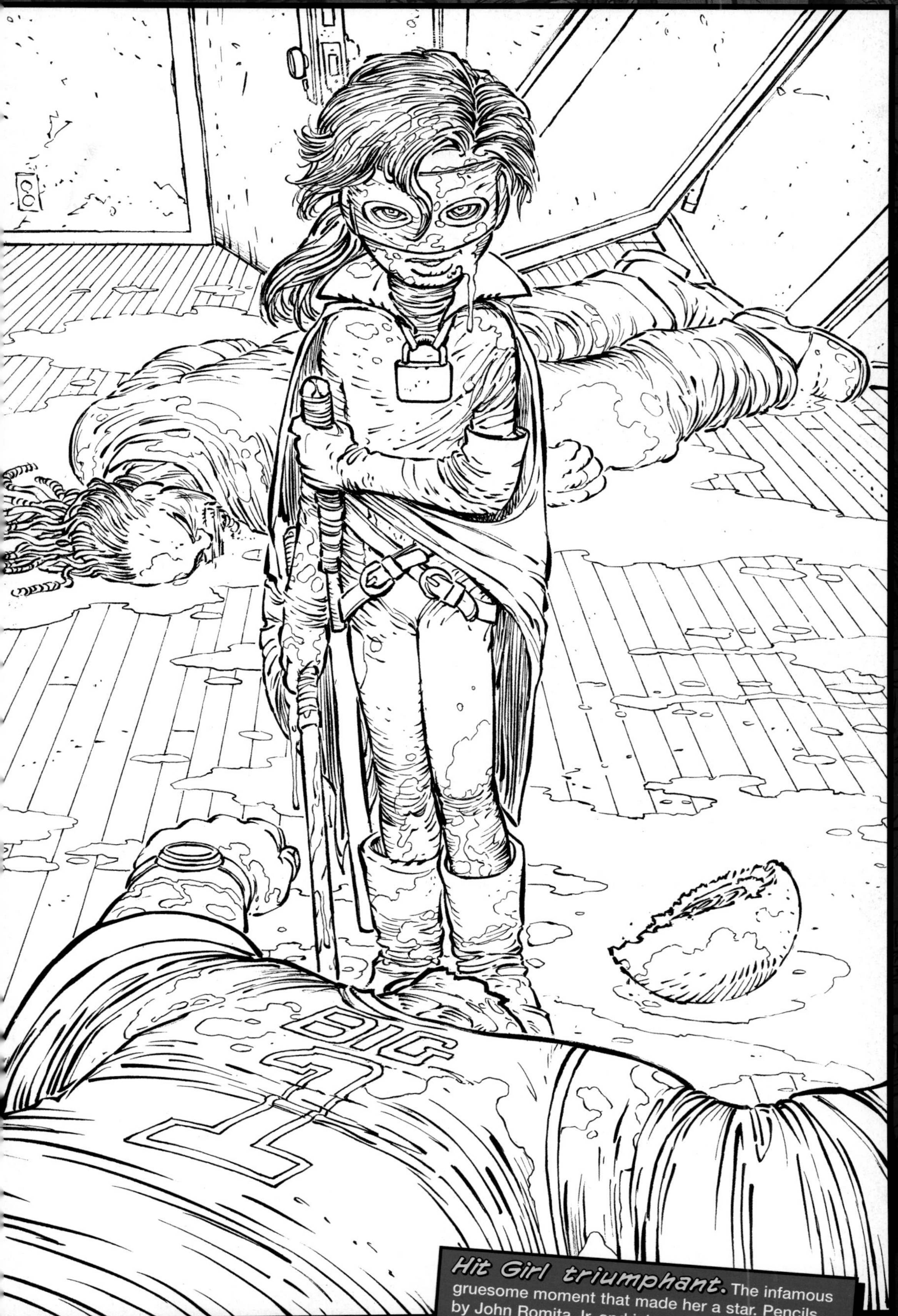
BIG
11

Hit Girl triumphant. The infamous gruesome moment that made her a star. Pencils by John Romita Jr. and inks by Tom Palmer.

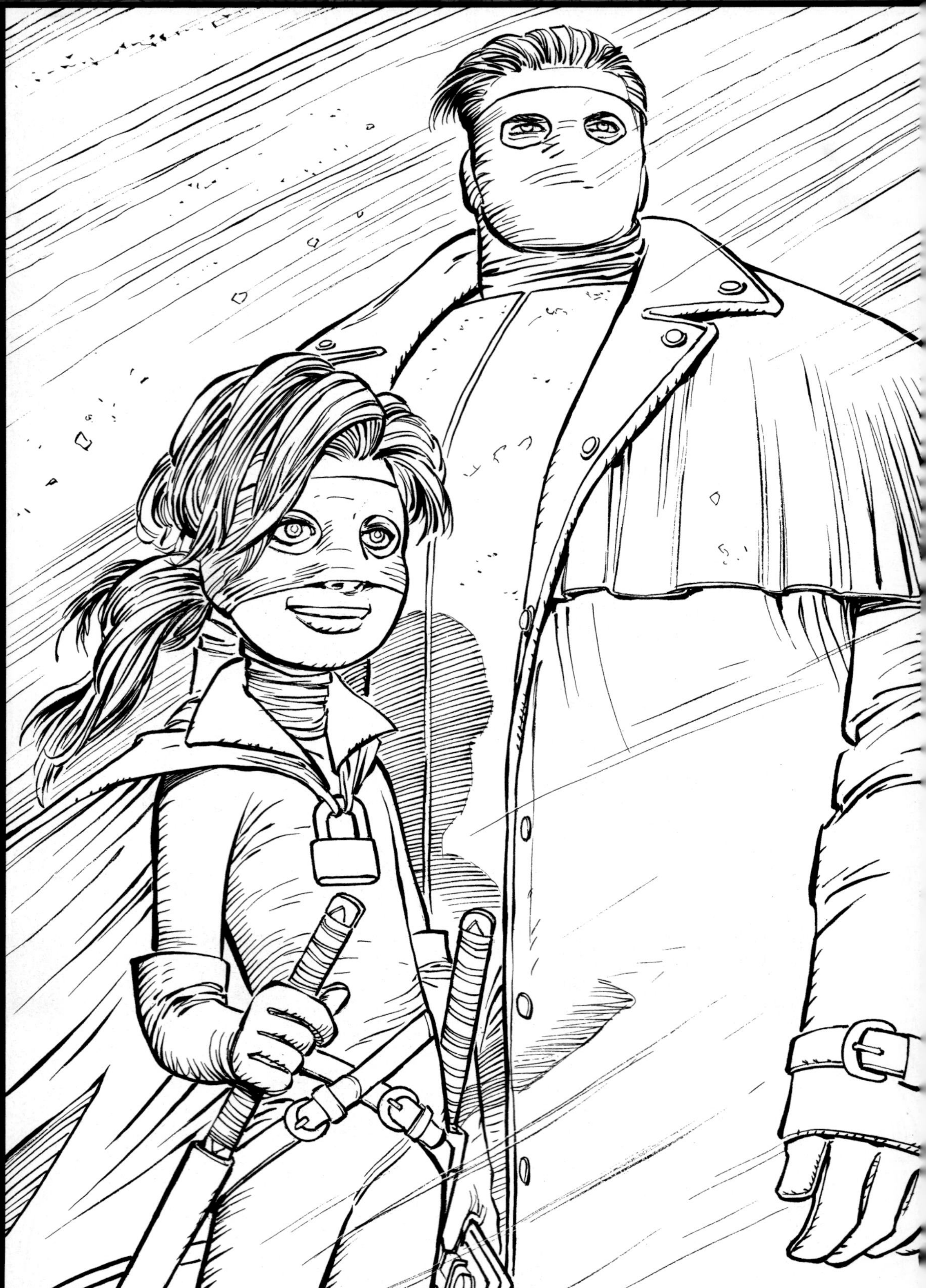

"Wotta fuckin' douche." Pencils by John Romita Jr. and inks by Tom Palmer.

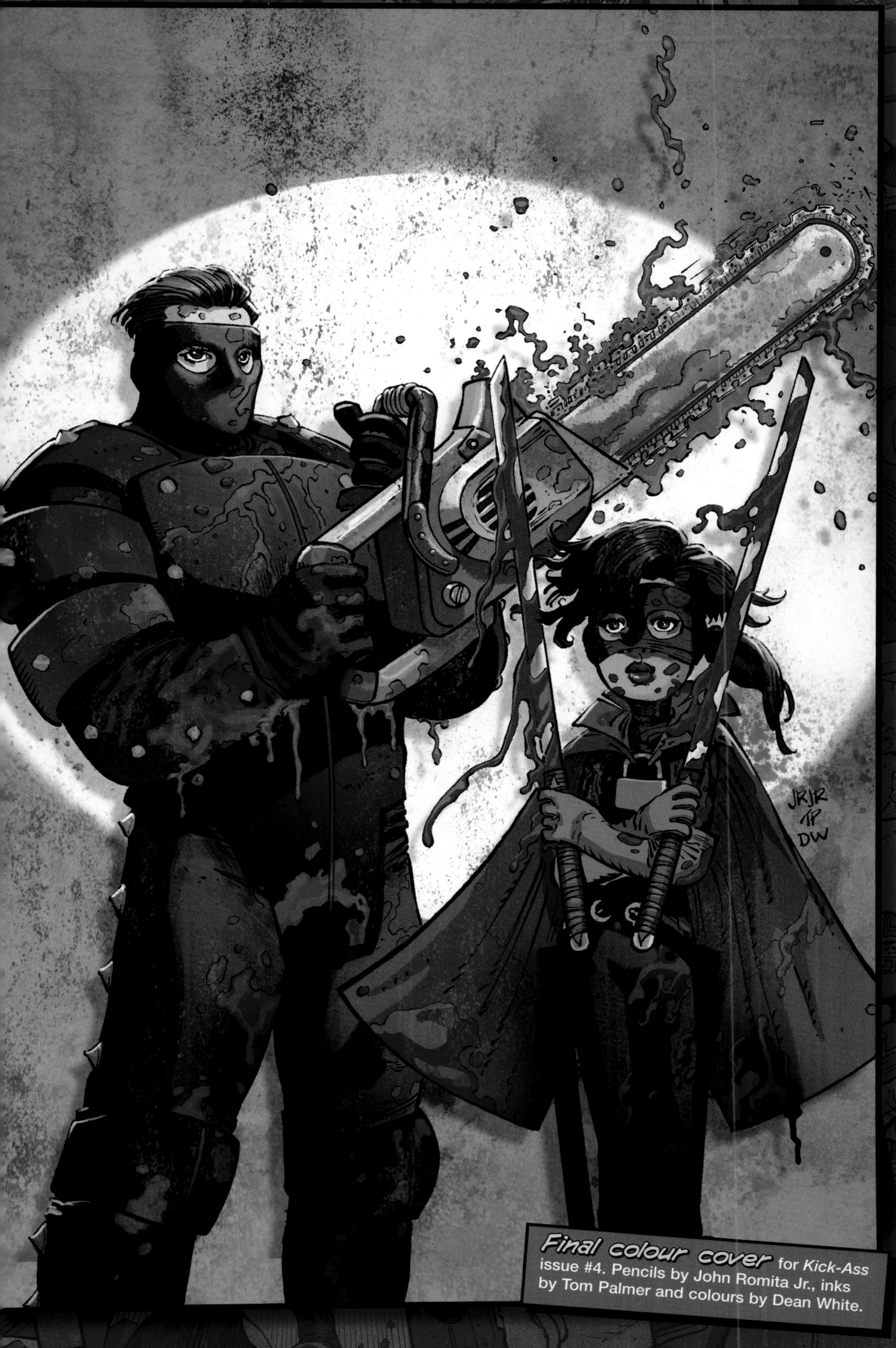
JRJR
TP
DW

Final colour cover for *Kick-Ass* issue #4. Pencils by John Romita Jr., inks by Tom Palmer and colours by Dean White.

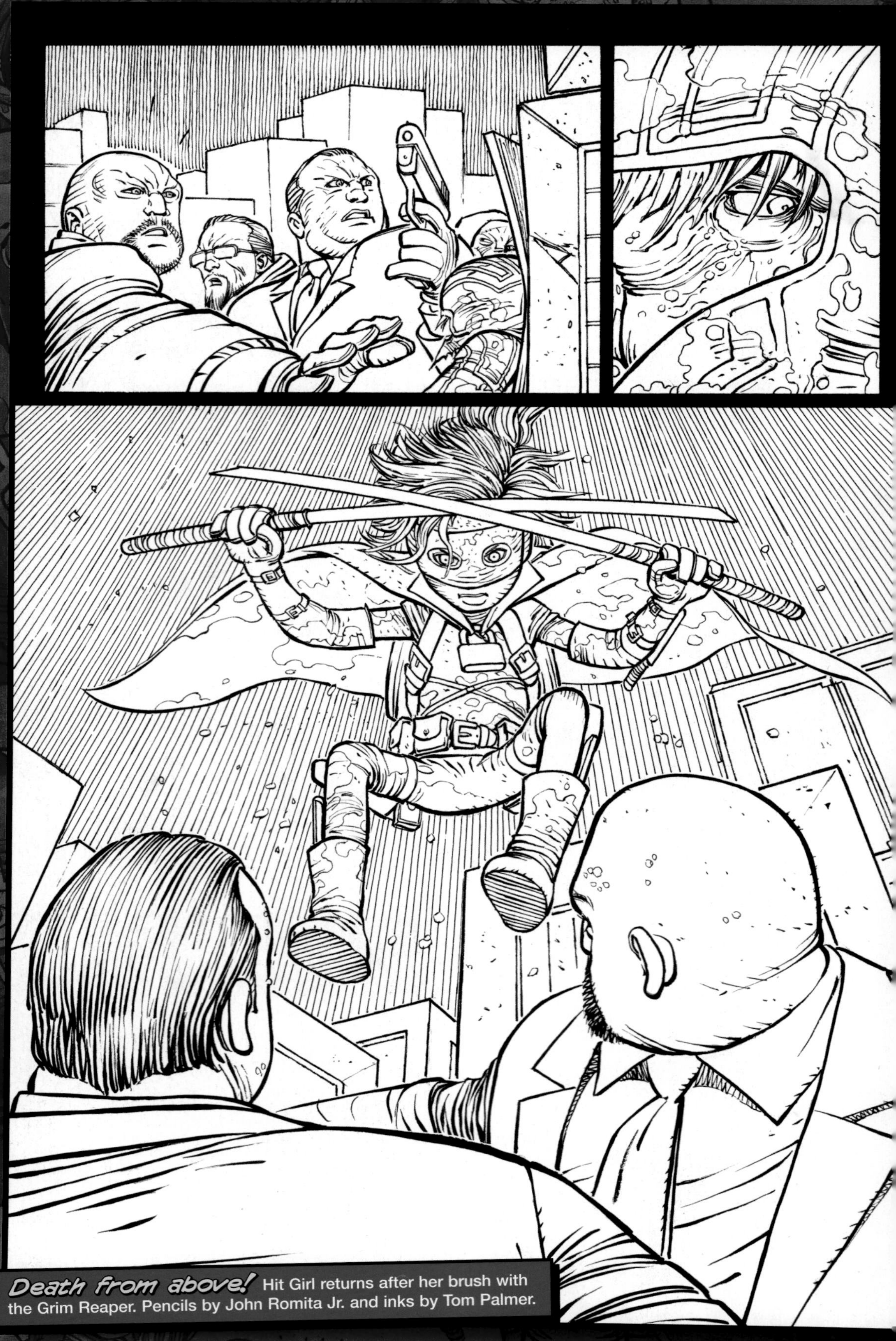

Death from above! Hit Girl returns after her brush with the Grim Reaper. Pencils by John Romita Jr. and inks by Tom Palmer.

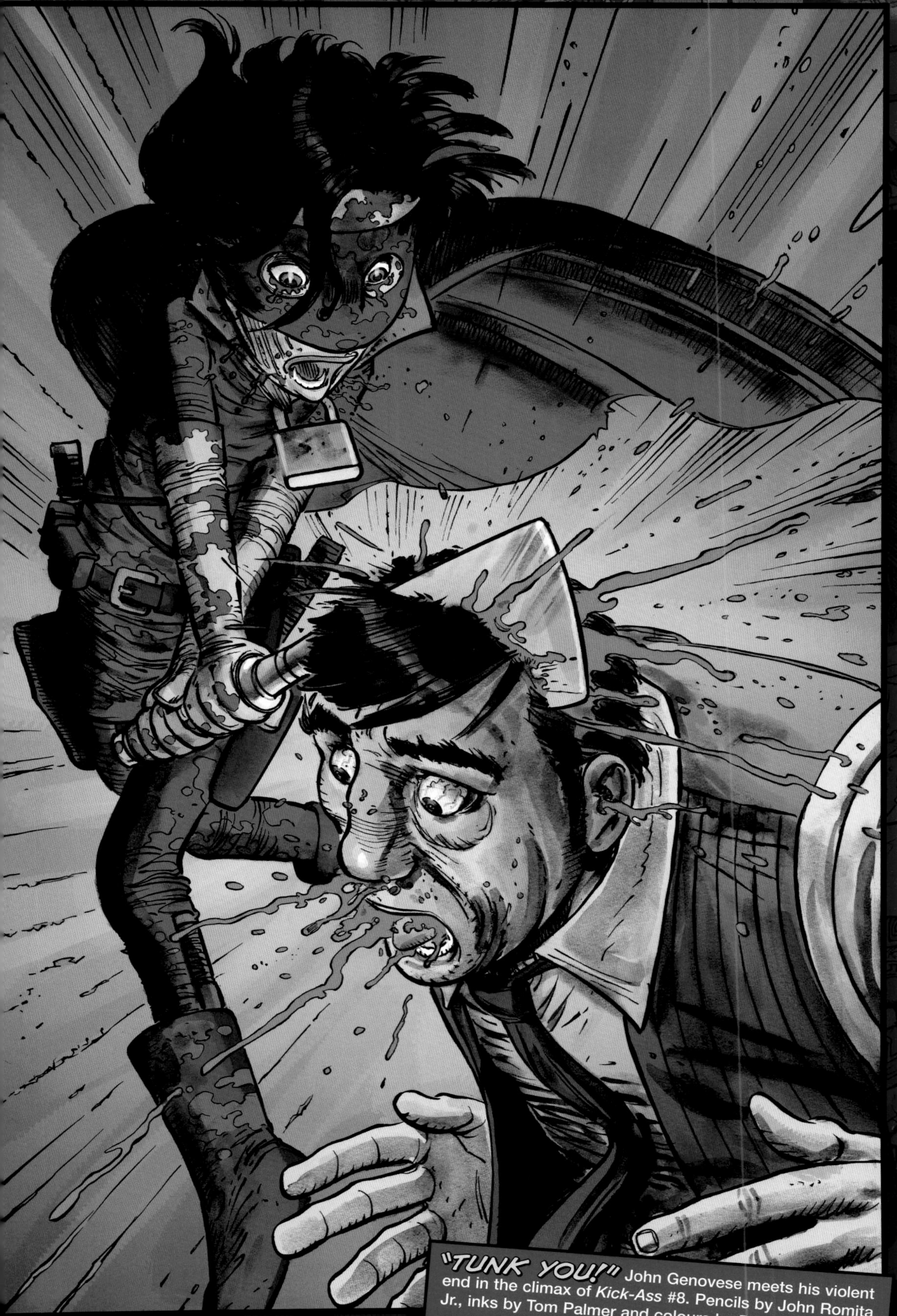

"TUNK YOU!" John Genovese meets his violent end in the climax of *Kick-Ass* #8. Pencils by John Romita Jr., inks by Tom Palmer and colours by Dean White.

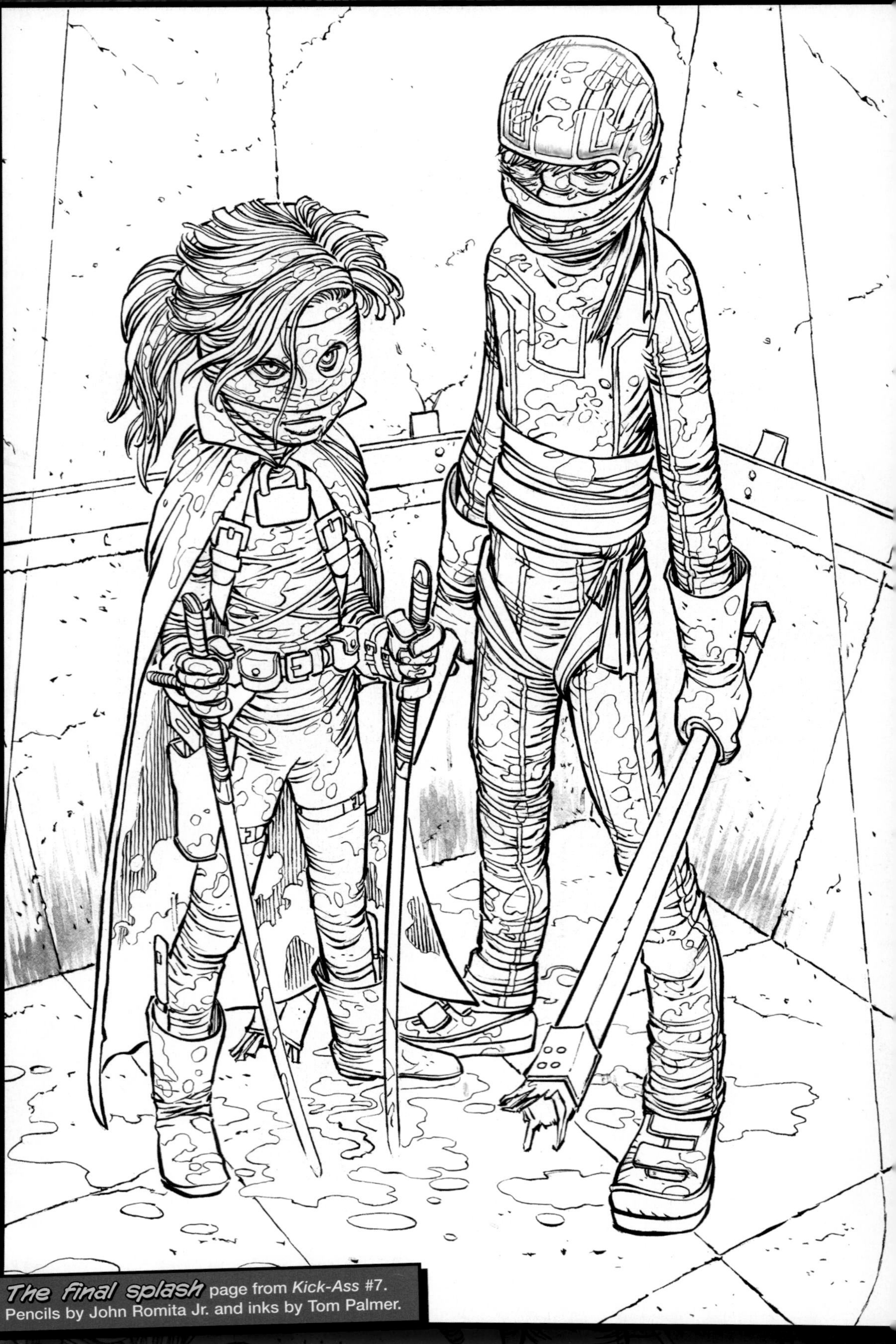

The final splash page from *Kick-Ass* #7.
Pencils by John Romita Jr. and inks by Tom Palmer.

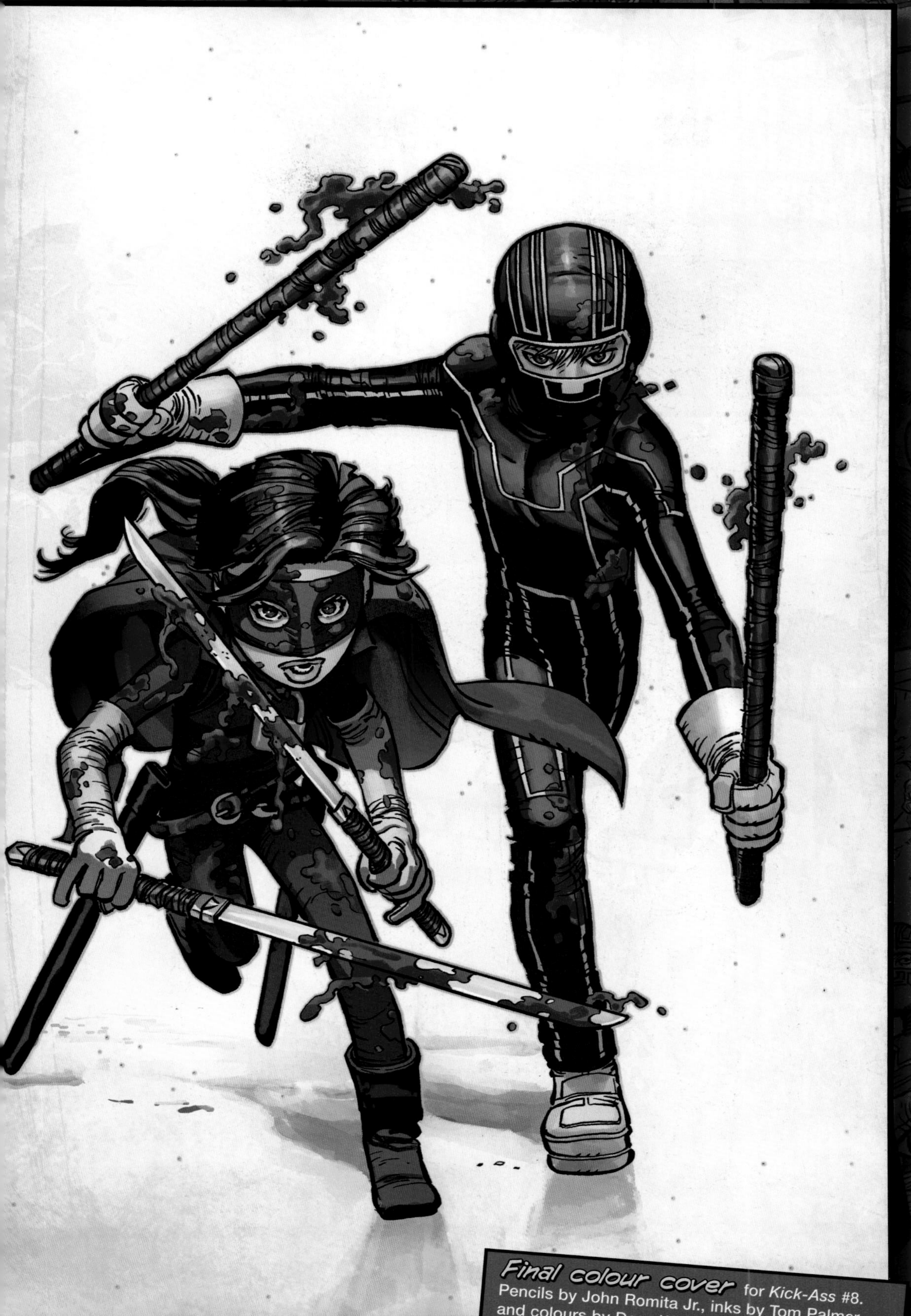

Final colour cover for *Kick-Ass* #8. Pencils by John Romita Jr., inks by Tom Palmer and colours by Dean White.

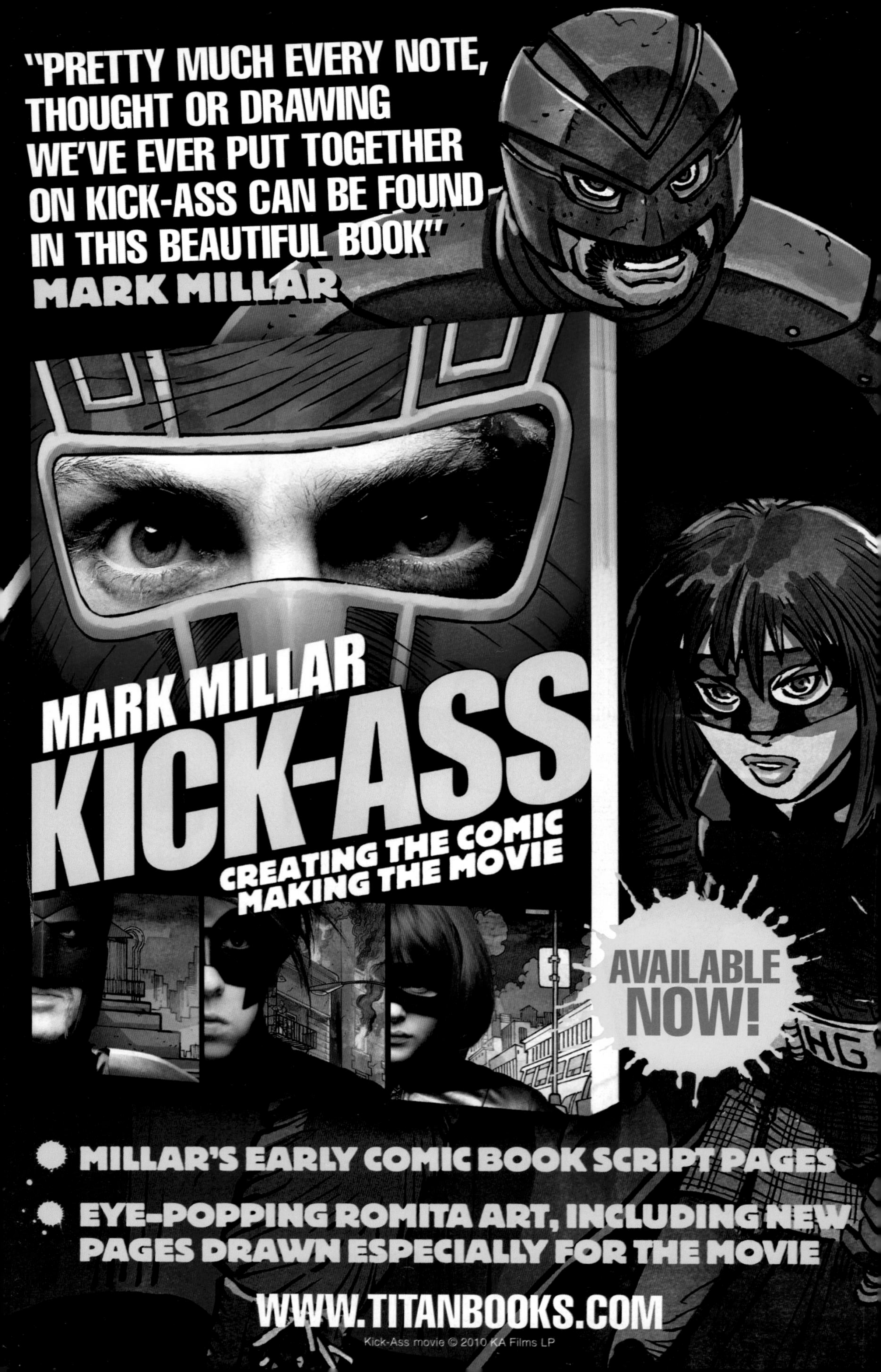
"PRETTY MUCH EVERY NOTE, THOUGHT OR DRAWING WE'VE EVER PUT TOGETHER ON KICK-ASS CAN BE FOUND IN THIS BEAUTIFUL BOOK"
MARK MILLAR
MARK MILLAR
KICK-ASS
CREATING THE COMIC
MAKING THE MOVIE
AVAILABLE NOW!
HG
MILLAR'S EARLY COMIC BOOK SCRIPT PAGES
EYE-POPPING ROMITA ART, INCLUDING NEW PAGES DRAWN ESPECIALLY FOR THE MOVIE
WWW.TITANBOOKS.COM
Kick-Ass movie © 2010 KA Films LP